# Qualitative Research Approaches for Public Administration

# Qualitative Research Approaches for Public Administration

## Larry S. Luton

*M.E.Sharpe*
Armonk, New York
London, England

**Library of Congress Cataloging-in-Publication Data**

Luton, Larry S., 1949–
Qualitative research approaches for public administration / by Larry S. Luton.
    p. cm.
Includes bibliographical references and index.
ISBN 978–0-7656–1686–9 (cloth : alk. paper)—ISBN 978-0-7656-1687-6 (pbk. : alk. paper)
1. Public administration—Research—Methodology. 2. Qualitative research. I. Title.

JA1338.A2L88 2010
351.072—dc22                                                                           2010018819

Printed in the United States of America

The paper used in this publication meets the minimum requirements of
American National Standard for Information Sciences
Permanence of Paper for Printed Library Materials,
ANSI Z 39.48-1984.


                                      ∞


CW (c)    10    9    8    7    6    5    4    3    2    1
CW (p)    10    9    8    7    6    5    4    3    2    1

This book is dedicated to my wife, Susan Hales. Our conversations about her work on her PhD dissertation initiated my reexamination of qualitative research approaches and resulted in this book. For that contribution to my professional and personal development (and for oh so much more!), I am very grateful.

# Contents

Acknowledgments                                                    ix

1. Qualitative Research Approaches and Public
   Administration Research                                          3
   What Is Qualitative Research?                                    4
   Qualitative Research in Public Administration                    5
   Why Public Administration Researchers Do
      Qualitative Research                                          9
   The Structure of This Book                                      14

2. Qualitative Interviewing Approaches                            21
   Designing a Qualitative Interview Research Project              26
   Preparing an Interview Guide                                    28
   Preparing for the Interview Situation                           32
   The Interview                                                   34
   Interview Data                                                  37
   Interview Analysis                                              41
   Composing the Manuscript                                        45
   Conclusion                                                      49

3. Narrative Inquiry Approaches                                   54
   Defining the Narrative Inquiry Approach                         57
   Why Narrative Inquiry?                                          59
   Design and Execution Challenges in Narrative Inquiry
      Research                                                     63
   Analyzing Stories                                               67

Composing a Text and Re-presenting Stories            73
Conclusion                                            81

4.  **Ethnographic Approaches**                       **85**
    Defining the Ethnographic Approach                87
    Types of Ethnography                              89
    Choosing an Ethnographic Approach                 90
    Design Issues in Ethnographic Research            95
    Logistical Issues                                 102
    Collecting and Creating Data                      104
    Analyzing It                                      108
    Writing It                                        112
    Conclusion                                        116

5.  **Qualitative Case Study Approaches**             **121**
    Defining the Case Study Approach                  122
    Kinds of Case Studies                             126
    Case Study Design Issues                          128
    Logistical Issues                                 133
    Collecting and Creating Data                      134
    Analyzing It                                      138
    Writing It                                        145
    Conclusion                                        153

Conclusion                                            157

Name Index                                            163
Subject Index                                         167
About the Author                                      173

# Acknowledgments

This book took a long time to write. The person who must have had doubts along the way but exercised much patience as I failed to meet our originally agreed upon deadlines was my editor, Harry Briggs. He was understanding and encouraging from the beginning to the end. Others who helped me keep at it included colleagues who asked to read early drafts of chapters and told me they hoped to assign this book to their classes when it was published—or gave me some other positive evaluation. Among those were Christine Reed (University of Nebraska, Omaha), Patricia Patterson (Florida Atlantic University), and Dragan Stanisevski (Mississippi State University). My students and colleagues at Eastern Washington University were supportive, as always, and put up with my lack of availability on my "research days." The completion of this book also depended upon the work of many colleagues who have demonstrated through their publications what serious, deliberate qualitative research approaches can contribute to the field of public administration. Finally, my wife, Susan Hales, who is accustomed to my somewhat deliberate pace on work projects, never questioned whether I would complete the task and was encouraging and helpful at several key moments in the life of the project.

# Qualitative Research Approaches for Public Administration

# −1−

# Qualitative Research Approaches and Public Administration Research

It is time for the field of public administration to take qualitative research approaches more seriously. This book is an attempt to help facilitate that transition.

For too long the field of public administration has been content to refer to any nonquantitative research as qualitative. Labels related to qualitative research have been applied to specific articles in public administration journals with little justification. For example, the "semi-structured interview" label has often been used to describe research based simply on extended conversations, but with no conscientious research approach in organizing or conducting those conversations. Similarly, the "case study" label has been applied to articles focusing on a short period in the history of an agency but without any systematic research approach.

Qualitative research approaches involve careful planning, respectful engagement, conscientious analysis, and deliberate presentation. For work to be based on a qualitative research approach, it is not enough for researchers to witness an interesting phenomenon, talk to some people, and then write their explanation of what happened and what they thought it meant. I do not mean to suggest that articles that are not based on a carefully planned and executed research approach cannot contribute to the field's understanding of the practice of public administration; however, just as an article that cites some statistics is not necessarily based on a quantitative research approach, an article that quotes from some conversations is not necessarily based on a qualitative research approach. Looking, listening, reading, and thinking may yield important insights, but without deliberate planning and execution, looking, listening, reading, and thinking do not constitute a qualitative research approach.

This chapter will begin with a section on defining what we mean by the term qualitative research approaches. It will then provide a brief review of the perspectives on qualitative research found in the field of public administration. Next, it will address why qualitative research in general is a valuable aspect of public administration research—what it contributes to the field. Finally, it will explain the plan of this book—how the book is organized to facilitate improved use of qualitative research approaches in the field of public administration.

## What Is Qualitative Research?

I am not very often impressed with attempts to establish specific denotative definitions for concepts that are utilized in varying but similar ways. Our common understandings of them are, in my opinion, constructed socially and are found in the areas of intersubjective agreement, not in strict adherence to a dictionary style denotative definition. Fundamental to my distrust of denotative definitions is the role that connotation plays in our understanding of concepts.

Nonetheless, a couple of the better attempts at defining qualitative research are found in the works of John Creswell (1998). He attributed the first to Charles Ragin, who distinguished quantitative from qualitative research this way: "quantitative researchers work with few variables and many cases, whereas qualitative researchers rely on a few cases and many variables" (1998, pp. 15–16). The second definition Creswell himself offered: "Qualitative research is complex, involving fieldwork for prolonged periods of time, collecting words and pictures, analyzing this information inductively while focusing on participant views, and writing about the process using expressive and persuasive language" (1998, p. 24). While this one adds significant aspects of qualitative research, it remains a rather idealized definition, not one that many instances of qualitative research would fully realize.

H.E. Brady and D. Collier have offered a third way of defining qualitative research. They identified four dimensions that can be used to distinguish qualitative from quantitative research: level of measurement, size of the N, the use of statistical tests, and thick versus thin analysis. Qualitative research is small-N research that relies on detailed knowledge of a small N rather than more limited knowledge of a large N. It uses nominal-level data, and verbal analysis rather than statistical analysis (2004, pp. 301–2).

Too often the term qualitative research has been utilized in ways that made it tantamount to "not quantitative." For example, D. Lowery and K.G. Evans operationalized qualitative research as "articles employing nonquantitative methods published in *PAR* from 1996 through 2000" (2004, p. 311). In my opinion their definition is too inclusive and may lead to misunderstanding. As the authors admit, their definition does not help to distinguish qualitative research approaches from other normative and expressive approaches (2004, p. 311). It is quite likely that some researchers whose articles they classified as qualitative do not understand themselves as doing research within a qualitative approaches tradition.

Defining qualitative as "not quantitative" also may feed the common complaint that qualitative research is so loose a conception that it is not possible to evaluate its soundness. Certainly, it is not fair to evaluate qualitative research by criteria established for quantitative research, but as E.G. Guba (1981) has explained, quantitative and qualitative research can be seen as having different ways of addressing similar criteria. Although qualitative approaches are not appropriately evaluated by their mechanical application of specific techniques, neither are those who use them completely free of expectations regarding accuracy, transparency, and integrity.

**Qualitative Research in Public Administration**

Almost every review of public administration research has found that nonquantitative research dominates the work in the field. H.E. McCurdy and R.E. Cleary found that only 15 percent of the dissertations categorized under the field of public administration in 1981 met standard quantitative social science criteria (1984). R.A. Stallings and J.A. Ferris examined the articles in *PAR* from 1940–1984 and found most of them to be "conceptual"; they discovered few causal analyses or tests of theory (1988, p. 583). In a review of the research found in a more recent decade of *PAR*, J.L. Perry and K.L. Kraemer found that the field's preference for nonquantitative research remained strong (1986,

p. 224). In 2000 Z. Lan and K.K. Anders reported on their review of the articles published in eight public administration journals in the period 1993–1995. They found that 40.8 percent used quantitative approaches and 58.7 percent used qualitative[1] research approaches. Most recently, in a review of public administration symposia, Miller and Jaja (2005) found a variety of qualitative and "other" approaches vastly outnumbered the quantitative approaches.

Many reasons have been given for public administration's resistance to being dominated by quantitative research approaches. Waldo identified the fact/value dichotomy upon which quantitative approaches rest as a basic problem (1948/1984). Some researchers have pointed to the applied nature of the public administration field and suggested that the field's major questions may not be well suited for quantitative approaches. For example, McCurdy and Cleary suggested "Trying to calculate with any degree of validity what constitutes 'good' administration may be an exercise in futility" (1984, p. 53).[2]

The positive reasons for utilizing qualitative research approaches in public administration have not been so well addressed.[3] Lowery and Evans (2004, pp. 318–19) present something of an exception to this generalization, but their case for qualitative methods was embedded within an article that focused more on a critique of qualitative research in public administration. In sum, their brief treatment of why public administration benefits from qualitative research approaches suggested that 1) those approaches are appropriate for addressing normative and ontological questions, 2) they foster good listening skills and reflexivity, and 3) they fit well with a view of the public administrator's role as a facilitator (rather than an expert).

Sometimes arguments for qualitative approaches have been embedded within a more general argument for diversity. Stallings, though he denigrated firsthand or "acquaintance with" knowledge, spoke in favor of including a mixture of quantitative and qualitative methods in public administration research (1986, p. 239). Jay White argued that "case studies, histories, descriptions of administrative experiences, reports of action research projects, political theories, philosophical analyses, and social critiques" (1986b, p. 15) could all contribute in important ways to the field's search for knowledge. Richard Box encouraged the field to be open to a variety of methodologies (1992). Guy Adams reminded us that public administration has a history of including a variety of research approaches and urged the field to welcome the contributions of historical, interpretive, critical, and qualitative research (1992). M.R. Schmidt (1993) chimed in with a clever metaphorical essay reminding the field of the value of alternative kinds of knowledge and the value of qualitative approaches. C.L. Felbinger, M. Holzer, and J. White recommended that doctoral students in public administration be "exposed to a broad and deep array of research designs and methods" (1999, p. 461).

Although public administration researchers have at times been generally encouraged to utilize qualitative approaches (e.g., J. Orosz, 1997), more frequently arguments in favor of qualitative approaches have been limited to specific qualitative approaches. R.P. Hummel made a case for narrative approaches (1990, 1991). Bailey defended the ability of case studies to contribute to our professional knowledge (1992). S. Maynard-Moody and M. Kelly argued for the use of interpretive approaches in policy analysis (1993). The 2005 series of articles by S.M. Ospina, J. Dodge, and E.G. Foldy (Dodge, Ospina, and Foldy 2005; Ospina and Dodge 2005a, 2005b) focused specifically on narrative inquiry.

Since 2000 the literature has also begun to address how well qualitative approaches are being used. R.E. Cleary (2000) reported on a replication of the survey he and McCurdy had done in the 1980s. While it was evident that he favored quantitative social science research approaches, Cleary conceded the value of interpretive and critical approaches. His main concern was that public administration researchers improve their methodological skills (2000, pp. 453–54). Similarly, R.S. Brower, M.Y. Abolafia, and J.B. Carr (2000) supported the utilization of qualitative research in public administration. Still, when they reviewed five years of qualitative research in leading public administration journals, they found the quality of that research lacking. To address that problem they made specific recommendations regarding how the field could improve its use and reporting of qualitative research. Lowery and Evans (2004) reached a similar conclusion and offered recommendations that were more focused on improving research methods courses in MPA and PhD programs.

In addition, a few public administration scholars have published qualitative research texts. H.J. Rubin and I.S. Rubin contributed one of the first texts in the field of public administration on how to do qualitative research (1995). That was followed by D. Yanow's short treatise on interpretive approaches (2000). In 2002 D.E. McNabb included four specific qualitative approaches in his text on research methods in public administration. Most recently, Yanow and Schwartz-Shea addressed basic epistemological issues, as well as particular ways of engaging in specific qualitative research approaches (2006).

The field is also producing research based on self-conscious utilization of qualitative approaches. Some work seems to come out of the interdisciplinary tradition of qualitative research (e.g., Z. Nedovic-Budic and D.R. Godschalk 1996; C.J. Cimitile et al. 1997; J.R. Thompson 1999; J.R. Sandfort 2003; P.M. Mareschal 2003; J. Kelly and J. Wanna 2004; D. Thatcher 2004). Others place their work in the interpretive, critical, discourse, and postmodern approaches frameworks (D. Silverman 1997; L.A. Zanetti 1997; M.A. Diamond and S. Allcorn 1997; A.J. Sementelli and R.J. Herzog 2000; A.D. Beresford 2000; F. Battistelli and G. Ricotta 2005). There is also work that is attentive to both the public administration qualitative tradition and the interdisciplinary qualitative tradition (e.g., S. Maynard-Moody and M. Musheno 2003; and Yanow 2003).

Another aspect of the discussion of qualitative research approaches in public administration involves the promotion of theoretical perspectives that fit well with those approaches. In the early 1980s Harmon (1981) delineated an action theory paradigm that has much in common with descriptions of qualitative research—intersubjectivist epistemology, attention to the meanings that actors ascribe to their actions, and an inclination in favor of engaged relationships between the researchers and the other subjects involved in the research setting. R.B. Denhardt's work has also demonstrated a position congenial to qualitative research—e.g., "I do not feel that theorists should spend all their time and energy working out supposedly causal relationships that may or may not be of importance in the real world. Theorists need to direct their attention to actual problems" (1993, p. 234). White and Adams made several of the key contributions to theory related aspects of research in the public administration field (e.g., White 1986a, 1992, 1999; White and G.B. Adams 1994). Their work has led to classifying qualitative approaches within public administration as either interpretive or critical. There has also been an interest in promoting normative theory in public administration (e.g., G.L. Wamsley et al. 1990; Wamsley and J.F. Wolf 1996; A.J. Sementelli and C.F. Abel 2000; Zanetti 2004). Some have engaged in advocacy for a qualitative perspective in conjunction with their attempts to give voice to marginalized persons (C. Stivers 2000; D. Burnier 2003; J.J. Hendricks 2003; M.H. Vickers 2003; J.R. Hutchinson and H.S. Mann 2004). Others have been leaders in bringing concerns related to postmodernism to the field of public administration (D.J. Farmer 1995; C.J. Fox and H.T. Miller 1995; O.C. McSwite 1996).

As this review of qualitative research in public administration shows, the field's research tradition has long included qualitative research approaches. Today our tradition of qualitative research is beginning to merge with the interdisciplinary qualitative research tradition. This should be no surprise, since public administration also has a history of interdisciplinarity.

While our field has not been very involved in the interdisciplinary conversation about qualitative research, it has its own tradition of qualitative research. In addition to using qualitative methods, researchers in public administration have engaged in significant discussions related to the theoretical perspectives associated with qualitative research. The remaining challenges include becoming more attentive to our use of qualitative approaches, learning to use them better, and reporting them more clearly.

In sum, qualitative research approaches are an important part of the public administration research tradition. The next question is, why is that so?

## Why Public Administration Researchers Do Qualitative Research

In general, there are two reasons why public administration researchers do qualitative research: (1) it helps us in our search for knowledge, and (2) it helps us engage personally and meaningfully with practitioners. There could hardly be a better pair of reasons for adopting an approach to research.

As has been shown, the field of public administration has a history of qualitative research approaches. This indicates that we believe a considerable portion of the knowledge we seek is effectively obtained through qualitative approaches. But why is that?

The kinds of knowledge we seek should be fundamental considerations in deciding how we conduct our research. Quantitative researchers seek an etic, nomothetic knowledge; based on an outsider's perspective, they seek laws, principles, and probabilities that they can generalize beyond the sample they study. Qualitative researchers seek an emic, idiographic knowledge; based on an insider's perspective, they seek understanding of a contextualized, specific situation, which may or may not transfer to other situations. This emic, idiographic knowledge can be very useful to public administrators. For example, the U.S. General Accounting Office[4] examined the use of ethnographic studies in the federal government and found that the insider perspective obtained through those studies assisted in improving agency programs, policies, and procedures (U.S. General Accounting Office, 2003, p. 1).

Such an insider perspective can be valuable in understanding the worlds of public administration practitioners, as well as the worlds of those affected by the work of public administrators. As P.M. Shields (2003, 2004) has argued in relation to the value of pragmatism for public administration, an approach that embraces "the practitioner's 'world of tangled, muddy, painful, and perplexing concrete experience'" (Shields 2004, p. 352, quoting James [1907]) is important in our field.

Public administration research also tends to recognize the importance of context, and qualitative research approaches contribute perspectives and insight on context that quantitative research cannot. In its quest for generalization and causal (or unit) homogeneity (cf. Brady and Collier 2004, p. 29), quantitative research diminishes the importance of differing contexts and attempts to find a generalizable causal model. In sharp contrast, McNabb suggests that case studies, for example, are particularly effective at presenting contextual factors, the interplay of individuals and collective institutions, of agency and structure (2002, p. 288). Public administration practitioners tend to be interested in context-specific answers, not cross-jurisdictional, national, international, or universal ones. They know that to some degree they are acting in unique circumstances, and they recognize that regional, cultural, and historical forces affect the transferability of answers from one setting to another. Public administration practitioners understand that generating revenue by placing a tax on tourist-related businesses such as hotels may be applauded in Orlando and vigorously fought in Fargo. Ragin describes this perspective as holistic, recognizing the situation in its whole complexity, "not as collections of parts" (1987, p. x).

One of the ways that qualitative research presents a perspective on complexity and contextuality that quantitative research cannot is through the use of thick description. Qualitative research uses thick descriptions instead of generalizable statistical analysis of data to reach conclusions. Composing thick descriptions entails intensive observation, notation, and interpretation. "Effective thick description brings the reader vicariously into the context being described" (David A. Erlandson et al. 1993, p. 33).

In doing so, it does more than report a lot of specifics. It involves the reader in grasping sufficient detail to be able to interpret those details, to be able to understand them almost as if they were there. The importance of involving the reader in interpreting the meaning of the specifics was illustrated by C. Geertz (1973, pp. 6–7) when he compared two boys contracting their right eyelids—one has a twitching eye and the other is winking. It is the interpretation of the observable data that distinguishes the twitch from the wink. The winker is communicating, an action that involves behavior in the context of human interaction according to a cultural code. Moreover, Geertz emphasized the importance of interpretation in thick description by extending the illustration to include fake winking and parody winking, both of which are distinguishable from the twitch and the wink by virtue of complex cultural, and contextually shared, understanding.

Public administration research is also enhanced through inclusion of the ways in which qualitative research addresses causation. Thick description is one of the ways that qualitative research addresses causation. Unlike quantitative research, qualitative research allows causal explanations to be understood as ideographic and emergent, as an unfolding of interconnected actions (Brower, Abolafia, and Carr 2000, p. 367). D. Collier, H.E. Brady, and J. Seawright (2004, pp. 252–55) have described this way of analyzing causation as "causal-process observation" or "thick analysis." Brady (2004) provided an example of the kind of improvement in understanding that thick analysis makes possible in his critique of John R. Lott's regression-based analysis of the impact of the media's premature declaration that Al Gore had won Florida in the 2000 election. Television news networks declared Gore to be the winner in Florida after polls had closed in the Eastern Time Zone (most of Florida) but before polls had closed in the Central Time Zone, which includes the Florida panhandle. Lott claimed that the networks had cost Bush at least 10,000 votes by causing Republican voters in the Florida panhandle to decide not to bother to go to the polls and vote. Examining the causal process, Brady critiqued Lott's claim by showing that the regression analysis failed to account for factors such as: the number of voters who intended to vote but had not yet voted when the networks declared Gore the winner, the number of potential voters who would have heard the networks' declaration, the number of voters who would have not voted based on that declaration, and the number of potentially affected voters who would otherwise have voted for Bush. Stringing together a series of calculations based on those factors, Brady concluded that the number of Bush votes lost was probably between 28 and 224.

Thick descriptions and thick analysis may not allow for confident predictions about what actions to take in order to obtain a specific result because they recognize a dynamic that Ragin calls "multiple conjunctural causation" (1987, p. 20)—outcomes that may result from several different combinations of conditions, making it difficult to identify a decisive causal combination. This dynamic is something with which public administrators are very familiar. For example, it may be a valid social science generalization to say that citizens' satisfaction is increased when the services they rely upon (such as police and fire protection) are delivered in a timely and effective manner, but that does not mean citizens will refrain from complaining if retaining adequate fire and police protection means that the hours of operation at senior centers have to be reduced. It is not a simple matter to identify the factors that affect citizen satisfaction, determine their loadings, and manipulate them to control citizen satisfaction. In specific circumstances, different factors have differential impacts in conjunction with each other and may or may not lead to citizen satisfaction.[5] There are multiple ways that factors related to citizen satisfaction may combine to promote satisfaction. In some settings a particular combination may work, but in others it may not.

As soon as the public administration conversation about research approaches began, some people contended that the field included both science and art. In this regard, one aspect of qualitative research that attracts public administrators is its appreciation of tacit knowledge. There are some kinds of knowledge that are difficult (perhaps impossible) to observe directly. Still, there is indirect evidence supporting that knowledge. Qualitative research approaches provide a valuable way of recognizing, understanding, and sharing such tacit forms of knowledge. In the literature of public administration we find important instances of the recognition and understanding of tacit knowledge. Mary Schmidt described this kind of knowledge as "a feel for the hole" (1993, p. 525) and said that it cannot be measured or represented by formulas—it is learned in the field and based on direct experience. In what is now a classic organizational theory article, S.D.N. Cook and D. Yanow (1993) described the role of tacit knowledge in organizational learning. In their study of companies making the best flutes in the world, they found that tacit knowledge gained in the workshop allowed flute makers to craft instruments sharing all the qualities associated with the kind of flute made by their company.

Another reason that public administration researchers value qualitative research is that they want to be there, to engage practitioners—both as the focus of their research and as the audience for it. As researchers in an applied field, we are inclined toward involvement with our subject matter. Qualitative research takes an engaged stance, not an abstracted one, in relation to public administration practice and practitioners. Moreover, qualitative research approaches offer distinct advantages to researchers seeking to engage practitioners in order to gain knowledge of and with them.

One of the key differences between qualitative research and quantitative research is the relationship that researchers have with those whom they are studying. Quantitative researchers proceed upon an assumption that they need to remain distant from the objects of their studies; theirs is an abstracted relationship. Qualitative researchers proceed upon an assumption that they need to be engaged with those whom they are studying; theirs is a situated and engaged relationship. "Qualitative researchers stress the socially constructed nature of reality, the intimate relationship between the researcher and what is studied, and the situational constraints that shape inquiry" (N.K. Denzin and Y.S. Lincoln 1994, p. 8). They use various qualitative interview approaches, ethnographic participant observation and analysis, and other approaches to get closer to the perspective of those they study (1994, p. 10).

M. Bolton and G. Stolcis argued that practitioners value case study research and common sense more than the scientific method; they work with data in a more qualitative fashion, using logic to generalize rather than adherence to quantitative methodological prescriptions (2003, p. 627). In 2003 R. Landry, M. Lamari, and N. Amara examined what determined whether academic research was used by government agencies. They concluded that practitioners' use of research depended not on which research approaches were used, but on the relations between the scholars and the users (2003, p. 203). This does not mean that all public administration researchers must use qualitative approaches, but it does indicate that the engaged stance may confer particular advantages for qualitative researchers in developing relationships with practitioners—relationships that will help add a valuable perspective to the field's understanding of public administration practice.

Another aspect of qualitative research approaches that some public administration researchers may find attractive is a willingness to advocate change (cf. C.S. King and L.A. Zanetti 2005). In the public administration research tradition, some of this kind of work has come out of the critical theory stream. Many public administrators are interested in initiating change in social systems and collective institutions. McNabb found evidence of at least five different approaches to action research in the public administration research tradition (2002, p. 364).[6] Although some may be less than enthusiastic about the direction in which a particular advocacy researcher has taken this approach, when public administration practitioners suggest that they are interested in research that helps them deal with a problem and helps them to take action to improve a situation, they are promoting an action research approach.

Finally, there are those in the field of public administration who want nothing more than to have their research be relevant to the experience of the practitioner. McNabb says that a key reason for doing case studies is to share with others what some public administrators are doing—to share noteworthy successes *and* failures (2002, p. 286). Streib, Slotkin, and Rivera (2001) expressed concern that those criticizing the nonquantitative research methods used in public administration were pressing an academic agenda and were not sufficiently concerned about the types of knowledge needed by practitioners. Bolton and Stolcis suggested that because the professional goals of scholars (publication and tenure) and practitioners (solving problems) are different, it is difficult to bridge the "gap between what practitioners expect and what academic researchers can deliver" (2003, pp. 626–27). Qualitative research approaches offer a way to bridge that gap, to enhance the possibility that public administration research will address topics of interest to researchers in ways that are relevant to practitioners.

**The Structure of This Book**

This book is an attempt to help public administration researchers begin to utilize qualitative research approaches in a more organized and deliberate fashion. It presents four of the more common qualitative research approaches used in public administration research—qualitative interviewing, narrative inquiry, ethnographic approaches, and case studies—in a way designed to help readers begin to use them. There are, of course, other approaches that might be included in a book of this sort, but these four involve most of the specific issues confronted in utilizing qualitative research approaches.

Each chapter on a particular approach is organized to:

- describe how the approach contributes to public administration research
- address definitions and variations in the approach
- introduce issues to consider in designing a use of the approach

The chapters also give advice on:

- preparing to engage with the participants in the research
- engaging with the participants
- managing data
- analyzing data
- composing manuscripts

Each chapter utilizes several articles to provide examples of how specific qualitative researchers have addressed the issues faced in implementing their research approach. Those exemplars, which are identified at the beginning of each chapter, have been made more easily identifiable by setting the authors' names in a special bold font, e.g., **Lyles and Mitroff**. You will gain more from my use of the exemplars if you read them prior to reading the chapter and then refer back to specific parts as I reference them in the chapter. The articles utilized as exemplars can be obtained through most university online journal databases.

The theory behind my utilization of the exemplars is that specific examples of the approaches in use will assist readers in obtaining a richer understanding of the challenges faced and the possible responses to them. No single article provides enough detail on every issue addressed, and there is not "one best way" to engage with the challenges faced in any qualitative research approach. I hope to assist researchers in understanding how to utilize these qualitative approaches, but I am very aware of the fact that each researcher must find his or her own way of doing them.

As there is no generally accepted denotative definition of qualitative research, so too is there no single recipe to follow in order to do it well. In harmony with the character of qualitative research, becoming skilled at it requires that you get a feel for the whole and understand that each research project will require you to modify your approach to fit the circumstances and engage respectfully with the participants.

## Notes

1. It is not clear how they defined "qualitative."

2. McCurdy and Cleary went on to suggest that public administration might need to change the kinds of questions it addresses and move on to issues that can be addressed using quantitative approaches.

3. There is, of course, an interdisciplinary tradition of qualitative research that contains many fine explanations of the positive contributions that qualitative research approaches make in other professional fields of study (cf. E.W. Eisner, 1991; C. Moustakas, 1994; Creswell, 1998; A.J. Vidich and S.M. Lyman, 2000; B.L. Berg, 2004). Because public administration scholars have not been significantly involved in the development of that tradition, this is not the place to review those explanations.

4. Since the referenced study was done, the General Accounting Office has been renamed the Government Accountability Office.

5. As T.J. Catlaw and G.M. Jordan (2009) have pointed out, it may in any case be a bit too much to expect to achieve citizen satisfaction. Public administration may be engaged more in trying to help people bear their unrequited desire for a preferred world that cannot be fully realized.

6. Of course not all action research is qualitative. Action research is often described as based on a pragmatic theory perspective that eschews the relevance of the quantitative/qualitative distinction.

## References

Adams, Guy. 1992. Enthralled with modernity: The historical context of knowledge and theory development in public administration. *Public Administration Review*, 52(4): 363–73.

Bailey, M. 1992. Do physicists use case studies? Thoughts on public administration research. *Public Administration Review*, 52(1): 47–55.

Battistelli, F., and G. Ricotta. 2005. The rhetoric of management control in Italian cities: Constructing new meanings of public action. *Administration & Society*, 36(6): 661–87.

Beresford, A.D. 2000. Simulated budgeting. *Administrative Theory & Praxis*, 22(3): 479–97.

Berg, B.L. 2004. *Qualitative Research Methods for the Social Sciences*. 5th ed. Boston: Pearson Education.

Bolton, M., and G. Stolcis. 2003. Ties that do not bind: Musings on the specious relevance of academic research. *Public Administration Review*, 63(5): 626–30.

Box, Richard. 1992. An examination of the debate over research in public administration. *Public Administration Review*, 52(1): 62–69.

Brady, H.E. 2004. Data-set observations versus causal-process observations: The 2000 presidential election. In *Rethinking Social Inquiry: Diverse Tools, Shared Standards*, ed. H.E. Brady and D. Collier, 267–71. Oxford: Rowman and Littlefield.

———— and D. Collier, eds. 2004. *Rethinking Social Inquiry: Diverse Tools, Shared Standards*. Oxford: Rowman and Littlefield.

Brower, R.S., M.Y. Abolafia, and J.B. Carr. 2000. On improving qualitative methods in public administration research. *Administration & Society*, 32(4): 363–97.

Burnier, D. 2003. Finding a voice: Gender and subjectivity in public administration research and writing. *Administrative Theory & Praxis*, 25(1): 37–60.

Catlaw, T.J., and G.M. Jordan. 2009. Public administration and "The Lives of Others": Toward an ethic of collaboration. *Administration & Society*, 41(3): 290–312.

Cimitile, C.J., V.S. Kennedy, W.H. Lambright, R. O'Leary, and P. Weiland. 1997. Balancing risk and finance: The challenge of implementing unfounded environmental mandates. *Public Administration Review*, 57(1): 63–74.

Cleary, R.E. 2000. The public administration doctoral dissertation reexamined: An evaluation of the dissertations of 1998. *Public Administration Review*, 60(5): 446–55.

Collier, D., H.E. Brady, and J. Seawright. 2004. Sources of leverage in causal inference: Toward an alternative view of methodology. In *Rethinking Social Inquiry: Diverse Tools, Shared Standards*, H.E. Brady and D. Collier ed., 229–66. Oxford: Rowman and Littlefield.

Cook, S.D.N., and D. Yanow. 1993. Culture and organizational learning. *Journal of Management Inquiry*, 2(4): 373–90.

Creswell, J.W. 1998. *Qualitative Inquiry and Research Design: Choosing Among Five Traditions*. Thousand Oaks, CA: Sage Publications.

Denhardt, R.B. 1993. *Theories of Public Organization*. 2d ed. Belmont, CA: Wadsworth.

Denzin, N.K., and Y.S. Lincoln. 1994. *Handbook of Qualitative Research*. Thousand Oaks, CA: Sage Publications.

Diamond, M.A., and S. Allcorn. 1997. Narcissistic processes and consulting to organizational change: A contemporary psychoanalytic perspective. *Administrative Theory & Praxis*, 19(2): 225–37.

Dodge, J., S.M. Ospina, and E.G. Foldy. 2005. Integrating rigor and relevance in public administration scholarship: The contribution of narrative inquiry. *Public Administration Review*, 65(3): 286–300.

Eisner, E.W. 1991. *The Enlightened Eye: Qualitative Inquiry and the Enhancement of Educational Practice*. New York: Macmillan.

Erlandson, David A., E.L. Harris, B.L Skipper, and S.D. Allen. 1993. *Doing Naturalistic Inquiry: A Guide to Methods*. Newbury Park, CA: Sage Publications.

Farmer, D.J. 1995. *The Language of Public Administration: Bureaucracy, Modernity, and Postmodernity*. Tuscaloosa: University of Alabama Press.

Felbinger, C.L., M. Holzer, and J. White. 1999. The doctorate in public administration: Some unresolved questions and recommendations. *Public Administration Review*, 59(5): 459–64.

Fox, C.J., and H.T. Miller. 1995. *Postmodern Public Administration: Toward Discourse*. Thousand Oaks, CA: Sage Publications.

Geertz, C. 1973. *The Interpretation of Cultures*. New York: Basic Books.

Guba, E.G. 1981. Criteria for assessing the trustworthiness of naturalistic inquiries. *Educational Communication and Technology Journal*, 29: 75–92.

Harmon, M. M. 1981. *Action Theory for Public Administration*. Burke, VA: Chatelaine Press.

Hendricks, J.J. 2003. Back to the future: Theorists as facilitators of voice, yesterday and today. *Administrative Theory & Praxis*, 25(4): 463–80.

Hummel, R.P. 1990. Uncovering validity criteria for stories managers hear and tell. *American Review of Public Administration*, 20: 303–14.

———. 1991. Stories managers tell: Why they are as valid as science. *Public Administration Review*, 51: 31–41.

Hutchinson, J.R., and H.S. Mann. 2004. Feminist praxis: Administering for a multicultural, multigendered public. *Administrative Theory & Praxis*, 26(1): 79–95.

James, W. 1907. *Pragmatism: A New Name for Some Old Ways of Thinking*. Cambridge, MA: Riverside.

Kelly, J., and J. Wanna. 2004. Crashing through with accrual-output price budgeting in Australia: Technical adjustment or a new way of doing business? *American Review of Public Administration*, 34(1): 94–111.

King, C.S., and L.A. Zanetti. 2005. *Transformational Public Service: Portraits of Theory in Practice*. Armonk, NY: M.E. Sharpe.

Lan, Z., and K.K. Anders. 2000. A paradigmatic view of contemporary public administration research. *Administration & Society*, 32(2): 138–66.

Landry, R., M. Lamari, and N. Amara. 2003. The extent and determinants of the utilization of university research in government agencies. *Public Administration Review*, 63(2): 192–205.

Lowery, D., and K.G. Evans. 2004. The iron cage of methodology: The vicious circle of means limiting ends limiting means . . . *Administration & Society*, 36(3): 306–27.

Mareschal, P.M. 2003. Solving problems and transformational relationships: The bifocal approach to mediation. *American Review of Public Administration*, 33(4): 423–48.

Maynard-Moody, S., and M. Kelly. 1993. Stories public managers tell about elected officials: Making sense of the politics-administration dichotomy. In *Public Management: The State of the Art*, ed. B. Bozeman, 71–90. San Francisco, CA: Jossey-Bass.

Maynard-Moody, S., and M. Musheno. 2003. *Cops, Teachers, Counselors: Stories from the Front Lines of Public Service*. Ann Arbor: University of Michigan Press.

McCurdy, H.E., and R.E. Cleary. 1984. Why can't we resolve the research issue in public administration? *Public Administration Review*, 44: 49–55.

McNabb, D.E. 2002. *Research Methods in Public Administration and Nonprofit Management: Quantitative and Qualitative Approaches*. Armonk, NY: M.E. Sharpe.

McSwite, O.C. 1996. Postmodernism, public administration, and the public interest. In *Refounding Democratic Public Administration: Modern Paradoxes, Postmodern Challenges*, ed. G.L. Wamsley and J.F. Wolf, 198–224. Thousand Oaks, CA: Sage Publications.

Moustakas, C. 1994. *Phenomenological Research Methods*. Thousand Oaks, CA: Sage Publications.

Nedovic-Budic, Z., and D.R. Godschalk. 1996. Human factors in adoption of geographic information systems: A local government case study. *Public Administration Review*, 56(6): 554–67.

Orosz, J. 1997. Resources for qualitative research: Advancing the applications of alternative methodologies in public administration. *Public Administration Review*, 57(6): 543–49.

Ospina, S.M., and J. Dodge. 2005a. It's about time: Catching method up to meaning—the usefulness of narrative inquiry in public administration research. *Public Administration Review,* 65(2): 143–57.

———. 2005b. Narrative inquiry and the search for connectedness: Practitioners and academics developing public administration scholarship. *Public Administration Review,* 65(4): 409–23.

Perry, J.L., and K.L. Kraemer. 1986. Research methodology in the *Public Administration Review,* 1975–1984. *Public Administration Review,* 46(3): 215–26.

Ragin, C.C. 1987. *The Comparative Method: Moving Beyond Qualitative and Quantitative Strategies.* Berkeley: University of California Press.

Rubin, H.J., and I.S. Rubin. 1995. *Qualitative Interviewing: The Art of Hearing Data.* Thousand Oaks, CA: Sage Publications.

Sandfort, J.R. 2003. Exploring the structuration of technology within human service organizations. *Administration & Society,* 34(6): 605–31.

Schmidt, M.R. 1993. Grout: Alternative forms of knowledge and why they are ignored. *Public Administration Review,* 53(6): 525–30.

Sementelli, A.J., and C.F. Abel. 2000. Recasting critical theory: Veblen, deconstruction, and the theory-praxis gap. *Administrative Theory & Praxis,* 22(3): 458–78.

Sementelli, A.J., and R.J. Herzog. 2000. Framing discourse in budgetary processes: Warrants for normalization and conformity. *Administrative Theory & Praxis,* 22(1): 105–16.

Shields, P.M. 2003. The community of inquiry: Classical pragmatism and public administration. *Administration & Society,* 35(5): 510–38.

———. 2004. Classical pragmatism: Engaging practitioner experience. *Administration & Society,* 36(3): 351–61.

Silverman, D. 1997. Studying organizational interaction: Ethnomethodology's contribution to the "new institutionalism." *Administrative Theory & Praxis,* 19(2): 178–95.

Stallings, R.A. 1986. Doctoral programs in public administration: An outsider's perspective. *Public Administration Review,* 46(3): 235–40.

——— and J.A. Ferris. 1988. Public administration research: Work in *PAR,* 1940–1984. *Public Administration Review,* 48(1): 580–87.

Stivers, C. 2000. *Bureau Men, Settlement Women: Constructing Public Administration in the Progressive Era.* Lawrence: University Press of Kansas.

Strieb, G., B.J. Slotkin, and M. Rivera. 2001. Public administration research from a practitioner perspective. *Public Administration Review,* 61(5): 515–25.

Thatcher, D. 2004. Interorganizational partnerships as inchoate hierarchies: A case study of the community security initiative. *Administration & Society,* 36(1): 91–127.

Thompson, J.R. 1999. Devising administrative reform that works: The example of the reinvention lab program. *Public Administration Review,* 59(4): 283–92.

U.S. General Accounting Office. 2003. *Federal Programs: Ethnographic Studies Can Inform Agencies' Actions.* Washington, DC: GAO-03-455.

Vickers, M.H. 2003. Chaos narratives to reinstate the voice of a survivor of mental illness: A (partial) life story. *Administrative Theory & Praxis,* 23(4): 513–28.

Vidich, A.J., and S.M. Lyman. 2000. Qualitative methods: Their history in sociology and anthropology. In *Handbook of Qualitative Research,* (2d ed.), ed. N.K. Denzin and Y.S. Lincoln, 37–84. Thousand Oaks, CA: Sage Publications.

Waldo, D. 1948/1984. *The Administrative State: A Study of the Political Theory of American Public Administration.* 2d ed. New York: Holmes and Meier.

Wamsley, G.L., and J.F. Wolf, eds. 1996. *Refounding Democratic Public Administration: Modern Paradoxes, Postmodern Challenges.* Thousand Oaks, CA: Sage Publications.

Wamsley, G.L., et al. 1990. *Refounding Public Administration.* Newbury Park, CA: Sage Publications.

White, J.D. 1986a. On the growth of knowledge in public administration. *Public Administration Review,* 46(1): 15–24.

———. 1986b. Dissertations and publications in public administration. *Public Administration Review,* 46(3): 227–34.

———. 1992. Taking language seriously: Toward a narrative theory of knowledge for administrative research. *American Review of Public Administration,* 22(1): 75–88.

———. 1999. *Taking Language Seriously: The Narrative Foundations of Public Administration Research.* Washington, DC: Georgetown University Press.

——— and G.B. Adams. 1994. Making sense with diversity: The context of research, theory, and knowledge development in public administration. In *Research in Public Administration: Reflections on Theory and Practice,* ed. J.D. White and G.B. Adams, 1–22. Thousand Oaks, CA: Sage Publications.

Yanow, D. 2000. *Conducting Interpretive Policy Analysis.* Newbury Park, CA: Sage Publications.

———. 2003. *Constructing "Race" and "Ethnicity" in America: Category-Making in Public Policy and Administration.* Armonk, NY: M.E. Sharpe.

——— and P. Schwartz-Shea, eds. 2006. *Interpretation and Method: Empirical Research Methods and the Interpretive Turn.* Armonk, NY: M.E. Sharpe.

Zanetti, L.A. 1997. Putting critical theory to work: Giving the public administrator the critical edge. *Administrative Theory & Praxis,* 19(2): 208–24.

———. 2004. Repositioning the ethical imperative: Critical theory recht, and tempered radicals in public service. *American Review of Public Administration,* 34(2): 134–50.

# −2−

# Qualitative Interviewing Approaches

One of the most basic ways of learning about something is to talk with someone who has knowledge about it. Talking with someone can take many forms, ranging from casual conversation to journalistic interviews to semistructured interviews to structured survey interviewing. It can be done with one person at a time or with groups of people (perhaps in focus groups). It may be done in a number of different ways. (For a particular variation—narrative inquiry—see Chapter 3.) Talking with people can also be used as a component of other research approaches, e.g., ethnography and case study approaches (see Chapters 4 and 5). Although there are some qualitative research projects that do not include interviewing, most qualitative research projects do. That is why this book includes qualitative interviewing as the first research approach it addresses.[1]

Qualitative interviewing, as it is being addressed in this chapter, is more deliberate in its design than most journalistic interviews, but it is sufficiently close to conversation that it has been described as "conversation with a purpose" (B.L. Berg 2004, p. 75). In qualitative interviewing, the purpose in talking with someone is "to learn about something in depth from another person's point of view" (H.J. Rubin and I.S. Rubin 2005, p. vii).

Qualitative interviewing differs from conversation in the degree of control over the structure and content exercised by the interviewer. The interviewer enters the interview situation with the purpose of better understanding a research problem and controls the interview to pursue that purpose. Often that control is embodied in an interview guide, a document

---

**Box 2.1    Exemplar Articles**

Baker-Boosamra, M., J.A. Guevara, and D.L. Balfour. 2006. From service to solidarity: Evaluation and recommendations for international service learning. *Journal of Public Administration Education,* 12(4): 479–500. Available through Education Research Complete (EBSCOhost).

Lyles, M.A., and I.I. Mitroff. 1980. Organizational problem formulation: An empirical study. *Administrative Science Quarterly,* 25(1): 102–19. Available through SOCindex with Full Text (EBSCOhost).

Okamoto, S.K. (2001). Interagency collaboration with high-risk gang youth. *Child and Adolescent Social Work Journal,* 18(1): 5–19. Available through Academic Search Complete (EBSCOhost).

---

that contains the themes and questions related to the research problem that the interviewer intends to have addressed. Qualitative interviewing differs from structured survey interviewing in the flexibility afforded the interviewer and the kinds of answers sought from the interviewees. Simple, brief answers are not sufficient. In qualitative interviewing, the interview is not seen as a pipeline for transmitting data but as a social encounter (J.A. Holstein and J.F. Gubrium 1995, p. 3). You are looking for explanations, examples, narratives, and stories about topics on which the interviewee is expected to be knowledgeable. You are seeking not just information, but understanding. As R. Connell explained her use of interviewing in research related to "gender regimes" in public sector organizations, it was to "go deep" (2006, p. 839).

When you "go deep," you are seeking to understand the perspectives of each of your interviewees, not only to summarize parts or aspects of a large number of interviewees' responses. R.S. Weiss (1994, p. 1) has pointed out, "Interviewing gives us access to the observations of others," to their interior experiences, perceptions, interpretations, thoughts, and feelings; it allows us to "learn about settings that would otherwise be closed to us." Therefore, despite the fact that you are asking questions related to your research problem to all of your interviewees—and you are probably working from some kind of basic interview guide that lists topics about which you intend to question your interviewees—in the end your questions are matched to your interviewees. In qualitative interviewing, the researcher enters the interview situation knowing that it will be necessary to ask for further examples and explanations to get the full story. Regarding this, Rubin and Rubin suggest that "even with a formal interview protocol in hand, you can ignore it if the interview follows a different path. If the interviewee anticipates later questions in their earlier answers, you simply skip the later questions" (2005, p. 147).

This structured but flexible approach to interviewing is sometimes described as semistructured interviewing. Research interviewing can be conducted in many ways, ranging from structured (aka, formal or standardized) to unstructured. Structured interviews are designed to elicit information by gaining short responses to predetermined and exactly worded questions, with no deviation allowed. Semistructured interviews are intended to purposefully pursue understanding (information *and* meaning), using predetermined questions, improvisational probes, and responsive follow-up questions. Unstructured interviews are wide-open, recorded conversations with no predetermined set of questions.

Semistructured interviews are often utilized in public administration research, because public administrators need to learn from the people they serve and from the people with whom they work in order to be effective. For example, E.J. Rossman (1992) reported that implementation of Superfund (an EPA program that funds and oversees the removal of dumped or abandoned toxic waste) required community relations plans, which led to the need for data from the affected community, which led to a decision to conduct interviews. Even though Superfund projects are highly technical affairs, the risks of a Superfund site need to be socially defined. Decisions about how those risks should be confronted should take into consideration the community members' views regarding the alternatives. Qualitative interviews are well suited to learning about the meanings members of a community attach to a risk and their perspectives on alternatives being considered.

There are many public administration topics that might be studied using qualitative research. The three examples of published research based on qualitative interviewing (see Box 2.1) that will be used for illustrative purposes in this chapter address a variety of topics: organizational problem formulation (**Lyles and Mitroff**), interagency collaboration

(**Okamoto**) and international service learning (**Baker-Boosamra, Guevara, and Balfour**).

As the three example articles demonstrate, there are also many reasons for utilizing a qualitative research approach (see Box 2.2). **Lyles and Mitroff** (p. 105) gave a very direct explanation of their decision to utilize qualitative interviews:

> Because many managers had not consciously reflected on the process by which problems were formulated, it was expected that they would need to be drawn out in a way that would not be possible with a written questionnaire. The semi-structured interview therefore seemed to be best suited to elicit the information needed, because it allowed for flexible questioning, explanation of questions that seemed unclear, and probing to help subjects become aware of their own problem-formulation process.

**Okamoto** (pp. 8–9) sought "to elucidate practitioners' perceptions, attitudes, and behaviors regarding interagency collaboration with a difficult-to-serve population." **Baker-Boosamra, Guevara,** and **Balfour** were engaged with Salvadorans in a service learning partnership and wanted to learn from their partners and include their voices in a way that further established "a relationship of honesty, reciprocity, and mutuality" (p. 479).

However, when an article says that it is based on semistructured interviews, it may or may not mean that the researcher did anything like what will be discussed in this chapter. Many academic research journal articles in public administration journals say that they are based upon semistructured interviews, but the authors often do not report enough about what they did in their research for the reader to discern whether the phrase refers to a conscientious use of a qualitative interviewing approach. Loosely organized interviews and conversations with people are not research approaches that fit within the approach to qualitative interviewing elaborated in this chapter. Rather, the approach this chapter describes involves conscientious, systematic preparation and careful, purposeful implementation. As this chapter will also show, successful qualitative interviewing requires more than effective mechanical application of techniques; it is a function of techniques and relationships.

In initiating these relationships, the researcher thoughtfully and purposefully selects the interviewees to include. Qualitative interviewing involves "choosing interviewees who are knowledgeable about the research problem, listening carefully to what they tell you, and asking

---

**Box 2.2    Reasons for Using a Qualitative Interview Approach**

(Based largely on Weiss 1994, pp. 9–11)

1. To better understand other points of view
2. To gain an insider's (emic) perspective
3. To understand the meaning that others attach to situations, settings, events, etc.
4. To understand their interpretations of those situations, etc.
5. To develop detailed descriptions
6. To develop holistic descriptions
7. To integrate multiple perspectives
8. To describe process(es)
9. To generate reflection by the interviewees
10. To build relationships
11. To combine with quantitative research for a more complete understanding
12. To explore a topic to better prepare for quantitative research

---

additional questions about their answers until you really understand them" (Rubin and Rubin 2005, p. vii). Responding to what you hear and asking questions based upon what others share with you requires improvisation—adapting quickly to the unexpected and listening not only to what you heard but also to what was skipped over or omitted altogether. Qualitative interviewing requires preparation, flexibility, careful attention, and genuine engagement. It is a meaning-making occasion that has been described as an active and creative encounter (cf. Holstein and Gubrium 1995; J.D. Douglas 1985; E. Goffman 1967).

Because this encounter involves an engagement with the interviewees that is more intense and more personal than is characteristic of quantitative survey interviews, qualitative interview practitioners tend to see their interviewees as partners in their research, not as subjects of it. A. Fontana and J.H. Frey have explained the reasoning behind this approach: "to learn about people we must treat them as people, and they will work with us to help us create accounts of their lives" (2003, p. 99). The partners, however, are not involved in equivalent ways because the researcher comes in with a purpose that guides the relationship.

Qualitative interviewing is a partnership that generates knowledge and understanding. It does not treat the interviewees as objectified sources of facts to be extracted by the researcher. The kind of knowledge that qualitative interviewing is well suited to facilitating is socially constructed —"created through the interaction of the partners in the interview conversation" (Kvale 1996, p. 11). All three examples utilized throughout this chapter recognized this aspect of their partnerships. **Baker-Boosamra, Guevara, and Balfour** referred to it as "the idea of mutual vision" (p. 481) and recognized that the concept of solidarity, which was very important to their Salvadoran partners, was not one with which they entered into the partnership. Both **Okamoto** and **Lyles and Mitroff** referred to their research as including aspects of grounded theory, the main characteristic of which is that it allows themes and concepts to emerge from the data. This means that their interviewees contributed to their research projects at the analytical as well as the data level.

Qualitative interviewing is an approach that involves the researcher in a partnership with the interviewees that not only entails the collection of data, but also the creation of understanding. The partnership develops out of social interaction that is centered in, but not limited to, the interview situation. The interview situation is more structured than a conversation, but more personal and interactive than a quantitative survey interview. Doing effective qualitative interview research requires a flexibility that is premised upon thorough preparation and careful design.

**Designing a Qualitative Interview Research Project**

Kvale (1996, p. 126) organizes the key design issues in qualitative interviewing around three questions: what, why, and how. *What* refers to pre-interview knowledge about the subject matter, i.e., the research topic that you expect to examine. As with any research project, you begin a qualitative interview research project by identifying a topic in which you are interested and refining that general topic into a more specific research question. It is what you know about a subject area that illuminates what you do not know and provides impetus to do research to address part of what you do not know—your research question. *Why* refers to the purpose of the interview(s). You interview people because you have reason to believe that they have experience, expertise, knowledge, and/or perspectives that will help you pursue answers to your research question. *How* refers to the approach you utilize in the interview. In qualitative interviewing, you utilize a semistructured approach that provides structure and flexibility and is organized to pursue a purpose, but is not so rigid as to prevent the interviewees from contributing new insights by presenting their perspectives in their own ways.

Since there are many research guides that describe ways to select a topic, develop a general research purpose, and formulate a set of research questions, I will not elaborate on that process here. Other issues such as selecting sites, interviewees, and interview questions in a qualitative interview research project deserve more attention here because they involve considerations sufficiently different from those encountered in other kinds of research projects.

Selecting an appropriate site includes two types of considerations, both of which are inextricably connected to the selection of interviewees. First, selecting an organization, program, event, etc., to use for your research may be the first way that you begin to place parameters around who might be selected as interviewees (or you might have interviewees in mind that lead logically to focusing on a site). Although the site has to be one to which you will be able to gain access, it should not be selected just because it is convenient. **Lyles and Mitroff** (p. 105) focused on upper-level managers representing a variety of functional areas from major private organizations, with over half listed in the Fortune 500. **Okamoto** (p. 9) chose to focus on a variety of agencies involved with high-risk gang youth. **Baker-Boosamra, Guevara, and Balfour** (pp. 486–87) interviewed eleven stakeholders in Salvador who had been involved with the service-learning program for at least three years and represented a cross-section of the program participants.

The second site-related consideration is where to conduct the interviews. It may or may not be helpful to interview people at the research project site or in their home. As the researcher, you have to make a judgment about where your interviewee will be most comfortable and most likely to talk openly and honestly. For example, because they were very conscious of the social context of interviews, **Baker-Boosamra, Guevara, and Balfour** conducted their interviews in different locations, "in places of the participants' choosing" (p. 488). The site-of-interview selection may be one of the first decisions that you and your interviewees make as partners in the research endeavor and is crucial in establishing the tenor of the relationship.

In qualitative interviewing, selection of interviewees is anything but random. It also should not be a simple matter of convenience. It should be quite purposeful. The main thing to consider in selecting interviewees is that they should have direct experience, first-hand knowledge, and/or a perspective you have reason to believe will be valuable. Sometimes the mix of interviewees is intentionally narrow to gain depth on a type of perspective. Other times it needs to be broad and differentiated to gain a variety of perspectives. It all depends upon your topic, the site of the research, and what you want to gain from the interviews. As was mentioned above, the authors of all three exemplar articles featured in this chapter had a purpose in the kinds of interviewees they sought and wanted variety among their interviewees.

As you decide upon your site and your interviewees, you will also be making decisions about which specific interview questions you plan to ask. The site, the interviewees, and the questions are key aspects of your research; the decisions you make about them need to be coherent and consistent. In qualitative interviewing, you need to be prepared to learn from your experience as you implement your plan and to alter your approach as you proceed. That kind of flexibility will help make the research project more effective.

**Preparing an Interview Guide**

You prepare the questions you are going to ask by developing an interview guide that includes topics to cover and questions to ask. Because of the need for flexibility in qualitative interviewing, it might be tempting to think of this research approach as one that does not involve a lot of advance preparation, but that is not the case. "The very openness and flexibility of the interview, with its many on-the-spot decisions—for example, whether to follow up new leads in an interview situation or to stick to the interview guide—put strong demands on advance preparation and interviewer competence" (Kvale 1996, p. 84). A typical interview guide would be organized by research questions that explore aspects of the research topic, primary interview questions connected to those research questions, secondary/alternative questions, and possible follow-up questions. **Baker-Boosamra, Guevara, and Balfour** developed an interview guide in both Spanish and English (p. 486).

The research questions are subtopics within the overall research topic. In their research into how organizations formulate problems, **Lyles and Mitroff** addressed four research questions:

---

**Box 2.3    Desirable Characteristics of Questions**

(Based largely on Berg 2004, p. 91)

1. Encourage participation
2. Elicit appropriate and useful responses
3. Are meaningful to respondents
4. Give the interviewees room to answer as they see fit
5. Contain an appropriate level of complexity
6. Utilize an appropriate style of language (e.g., vernacular or professional)

---

1. How do organizations become aware of the existence of problems and in what kinds of problems is the process important?
2. What process do organizations go through to formulate definitions of problems?
3. What impact do attitudes and demographic characteristics of individual managers have upon the problem-formulation process?
4. What are some of the major emergent themes that characterize problem formulation in organizations? (p. 102)

**Okamoto's** research questions addressed "the purpose of interagency collaboration, the elements contributing to successful interagency collaboration and the elements that negatively impacted interagency collaboration" (p. 10). **Baker-Boosamra, Guevara, and Balfour** were looking for "reasons for and benefits of participation, program criticism, and suggestions for improving the program" (p. 489).

The phrasing of the actual questions to be asked during the interview requires careful attention. Berg has indentified both desirable and undesirable characteristics of interview questions (see Boxes 2.3 and 2.4). Some people who conduct qualitative interviews believe the questions should be kept simple and brief (e.g., Kvale 1996, p. 132), but others worry less about the exact wording of the questions and focus on engaging the interviewees in a manner that encourages them to talk on the subject matter in whatever way they choose (e.g., Weiss 1994; Beebe 2001).

Often the primary interview questions are limited in number (probably 3–6) and translate "the research topic into terms that the interviewee can relate to and discuss" (Rubin and Rubin 2005, p. 135). Secondary/alternative questions tend to be more specific and can be utilized if an

---

**Box 2.4   Undesirable Characteristics of Questions**

(Based largely on Berg 2004, p. 91)

1. Encourages yes/no (or other very short) answers

2. Indicates your own leanings

3. Affectively loaded

4. Double-barreled

5. Threatening or unsettling

6. Vague or multiple meaning

---

interviewee anticipates some of the primary questions, making them unnecessary. **Lyles and Mitroff** (pp. 105–6) first asked their interviewees to identify a significant problem impacting the whole organization. Then they asked when and how the interviewees had become aware of the problem and what they did as a result. Finally, they asked additional questions about things that influenced the problem-formulation process and how their interviewees resolved differences in perspectives on the problem. Using a different approach, **Okamoto** constructed an interview guide based on an inverted funnel sequence, "where each new question had a wider scope than the preceding one" (2001, p. 10); consequently, the primary questions about agency policy and administration and recent innovations impacting the collaborative process came at the end. **Baker-Boosamra, Guevara, and Balfour** organized their semistructured interview by using twelve open-ended questions (see their Table 2) that were supplemented by improvised probes.

Probes and follow-up questions serve a similar function—developing richer, more detailed interviews by encouraging interviewees to tell you more on a topic. They can be used to get interviewees to expand on something they have said, to fill in details, to identify actors, to get them to verbalize a nonverbal gesture or sound, and to explore their inner thoughts and feelings. The term *probe* is sometimes limited to nonverbal or formulaic verbal encouragements (see Box 2.5). Follow-up questions, then, would be more specific and tailored verbal requests for additional information.

Follow-up questions are used in response to specific comments made by the interviewees, so their use depends upon what the interviewee says. They show that you are paying attention and give you opportunities to explore and clarify aspects of the interviewee's comments. Weiss

| Box 2.5    Examples of Probes |
| --- |

1. Why do you say that?

2. Could you tell me about a time when . . . ?

3. Is there a specific incident that . . . ?

4. Could you tell me what happened from the beginning?

5. How did that start?

6. What led to that?

7. Could you go on with that?

8. What happened next?

9. Could you walk me through that?

10. Who else was there?

11. Did you talk to anyone about that?

12. What thoughts did you have?

13. What were your feelings?

describes a particular kind of comment that calls for a follow-up question as a "marker," which he defines as "a passing reference made by a respondent to an important event or feeling state" (1994, p. 77). The passing reference usually is accompanied by some nonverbal cues that it holds significant meaning and/or is loaded with strong feelings for the interviewee. Weiss recommends that you note a marker and return to it as soon as possible. Prior to asking a follow-up question, it sometimes it helps to summarize what was said earlier (what you are following up on). Follow-ups may be used to pursue new ideas, to seek missing information, to seek stories or some other kind of elaboration, or to test the limits of something said earlier—for example, seeking exceptions to a generalization asserted in the interview. Being prepared is the key to asking good follow-up questions, but you cannot follow up on everything, so judicious use will help you get the most out of them.

Being prepared for the interview means more than having developed an organized research guide, knowing how to use probes, and knowing when and how to follow up. You also need to be prepared for the interview situation, the heart of your engagement with your interview partners.

**Preparing for the Interview Situation**

Preparing for the interview includes anticipating ethical issues, honing your interview approach, contacting your prospective interviewees, helping to make them comfortable, and facilitating your own comfort. **Baker-Boosamra, Guevara, and Balfour** had a university liaison make the initial contacts with their Salvadoran interviewees (p. 486).

Prior to beginning interviews, you need to prepare a consent form. When you meet with interviewees, you should have two copies—one for the interviewee to sign for your files and one for the interviewee to keep. Although consent forms are often designed in response to the requirements of an Internal Review Board, they should be seen as representing your respect for the interviewees in your research partnership. Obtaining consent is more a matter of ethics and respect than one of bureaucratic or legal rules. Although obtaining consent, and specifying what is being consented to, is central to the consent form, it should also address such issues as the interviewee's right to privacy, his/her right to withdraw from the project at any time, your obligation to try to protect the interviewee from any harm that might result from his/her participation, whether (and if so how) you will protect his/her confidentiality, and whether you will allow the interviewee to review your report prior to publication (also, perhaps, specifying the degree of editorial control, if any, interviewees have over the report). **Baker-Boosamra, Guevara, and Balfour** mention sending a letter explaining the research project and requesting participation (p. 486), but they do not address their use of a consent form. (For further information on consent forms, I recommend Weiss, 1994, Appendix D, pp. 214–18.)

Because a qualitative interview is both a search for information on a research topic and a social interaction, prior to conducting your first interview it is wise to have someone with expertise in the area perform a subject matter review of the guide and to do some practice or pilot interviews. You need to have given some thought to presenting the questions so that they facilitate development of the relationship you are creating and promote personal engagement. You either might have friends or colleagues take on the role of an interviewee to test drive the interview approach you have designed, or you might simply begin by interviewing people who are not central to your project so that if you make serious mistakes you may learn from them without jeopardizing the entire project. Berg (2004, p. 118) suggests that you keep your practice interview sessions short.

---

**Box 2.6    Things to Tell Interviewees on First Contact**

(Based on Weiss 1994, p. 35)

1. Who you are
2. Reasons for the study
3. Who (if anyone) is sponsoring the study
4. How you got his/her name
5. Why s/he was selected
6. Purpose of the interview
7. What (in general) will be asked
8. Whether and how confidentiality will be protected; and
9. Whether and how the interview will be recorded

---

Because the interview partnership entails developing a relationship, it would be helpful to meet with interviewees prior to the interview session in order to brief them on such issues as the purpose of the interview, how it will be conducted, and what will happen afterward. This might also be a good time to present them with the consent form. That would give them a chance to think about it and help you avoid setting a warning tone at the beginning of the interview session. You might lose some potential interviewees between the initial briefing meeting and the planned interview session, but you do want to be confident that they are willing participants in the partnership. Genuine informed consent may require time for reflection.

Even if you do not have a pre-interview briefing, you are quite likely going to have some kind of contact with the interviewees prior to the interview. In order to recruit them for the interview, you will probably have to introduce yourself, describe your study, tell them how you obtained their name (and/or why they were selected), and describe the interview process (see Box 2.6). First impressions are crucial, so do not hesitate to sell yourself and your study. Try to establish some common ground, e.g., network overlaps, mutual friends, and/or other things with which you both may be familiar. Being open, honest, fair, and accepting can help to establish trust and build comfort. Explain why the interviewee might want to participate—e.g., getting his/her story told. Make sure the interviewees know that you value what they have to say, that you

---

**Box 2.7   Berg's Ten Commandments of Interviewing**

(2004, pp. 110–11)

1. Never begin an interview cold
2. Remember your purpose
3. Present a natural front
4. Demonstrate aware hearing
5. Think about your appearance
6. Interview in a comfortable place
7. Don't be satisfied with monosyllabic answers
8. Be respectful
9. Practice, practice, and practice some more
10. Be cordial and appreciative

---

will respect their time by not demanding too much of it, and that you will schedule the interview at a time and in a place that is convenient and comfortable for them. **Baker-Boosamra, Guevara, and Balfour** explicitly mention respect as a reason that they allowed their interviewees to select the places where the interviews took place (p. 488).

**The Interview**

It might be helpful to think of the interview as composed of three sections: the pre-interview conversation, the actual interview, and the post-interview conversation. (Each one, of course, could be done in multiple parts.)

Berg says that you should never begin an interview cold. Chatting and making small talk help both of you to become more comfortable. You also should precede the actual interview by briefly reviewing the consent form and discussing the research project, making sure the interviewee has an opportunity to raise any remaining questions about its purpose and your plans for dissemination.

Your most obvious role during the interview is as a respectful listener. You want to talk enough to guide the interview, but you reduce your opportunity to learn from your interviewees if you talk too much. Your purpose is to encourage the interviewee to talk in ways that assist your research, so you keep your interview guide in mind and you ask for specifics, clarification, and meaning—more details, the identities of players, what the interviewee

---

**Box 2.8    Signs That an Interview Is Going Well**

1. The answers provide rich, nuanced, and vivid depth, detail, and meaning
2. Interviewees suggest lines of questioning
3. Interviewees anticipate your questions
4. Interviewees point out subtleties you might have missed
5. You can identify "iconic" moments
6. You feel absorbed and excited
7. You discover important questions that you did not anticipate
8. Interviewees say, "This is fun!"

---

noticed, thought, and felt. During the interview Berg suggests being purposeful, attentive, patient, cordial, and appreciative but probing. (See Box 2.7.)

As has been emphasized earlier in this chapter, qualitative interviewing involves developing and nurturing a relationship. For that reason, I do not recommend telephone interviews. Terry Gross suggests that they make it easier to ask challenging questions (2004 p. xviii), but that ease is a function of the shallower connection that the telephone allows between you and your interviewee. Telephone conversations do not allow you to see the nonverbal cues given by the interviewee, and it is harder to tell whether questions are sensitive to him/her. As a result, you will have a more difficult time engaging and building trust, and the interviewee may be more evasive, more cautious. Still, you may have to resort to telephone interviews for reasons of economy (time and/or money). As Jane Tausig and Ellen Freeman have said, telephone interviews are the "next best thing to being there" (quoted in Weiss 1994, p. 59).

Part of nurturing the interviewing relationship involves not wearing out your welcome. In addition, you do not want to wear yourself (or your interviewee) out. An interview that goes on too long will reduce your ability to be alert and attentive. Interviewing can be exhilarating and exciting, but because you are getting into someone else's world, it can be disorienting and generate overwhelming thoughts and feelings. So, for the sake of both the interviewer and the interviewee, you may need to schedule more than one interview session. Moreover, you do not want to schedule very many interviews in a single day.

| Box 2.9   Signs That an Interview Is Not Going Well |
| --- |
| 1.  Neither you nor the interviewee is relaxed |
| 2.  You find it difficult to pay close attention |
| 3.  Your questions are awkward |
| 4.  Interviewees appear puzzled by the questions |
| 5.  Interviewees express dismay or dissatisfaction with the experience |

You also do not want to leave your partners with post-interview anxieties. Certainly the way you conduct yourself at the interview—being tactful, sympathetic, and understanding—can help with that. Weiss describes the role of the interviewer as a "respectful student" and says you need to be "serious, respectful, [and] interested" (1994, pp. 8 and 66). A debriefing session after the interview can also help, but if that is not feasible some kind of contact or communication after the interview will help the interviewees deal with potential problems such as feelings of abandonment or the need to share with someone their post-interview reflections. The continued contact involved in their editorial review of the report may be sufficient for some interviewees, but others may need more post-interview attention.

Finally, the preceding paragraphs may seem to imply that you can always trust your interviewees, but they may resort to evasion, omission, or deception when asked about sensitive issues. Exaggeration and fabrication are often used to present a favorable image—of oneself or of one's organization, association, group, or community. Rubin and Rubin suggest that you should not get upset if you catch someone deceiving you: "Instead back off and rethink why the lie occurred" (2005, p. 72). There is no benefit in embarrassing your interviewee—or yourself. People are going to use official stories as self-serving fronts, but those official stories can often be identified by their superficiality. "When a respondent wants you to believe something that is different from what actually happened, the respondent is likely to avoid providing detail and to frustrate your efforts to elicit detail" (Weiss 1994, p. 142). You can also sort out deception by asking the same question in different ways or to different people, or otherwise comparing an interviewee's answer to some other sources.

During the actual interview, however, you need to find ways to probe respectfully. Terry Gross, the host of the National Public Radio interview

---

**Box 2.10    Things to Avoid While Interviewing**

(Based on Weiss 1994, pp. 78–79)

1. Talking too much
2. Interrupting
3. Finishing your interviewee's sentences
4. Suggesting phrasings for your interviewee
5. Offering your own associations
6. Suggesting explanations
7. Insisting on completing your questions when the interviewee has begun to talk
8. Talking about yourself too much (but some self-disclosure is vital)
9. Following your own preset schedule (or any other pattern) without paying attention to your interviewee's train of thought
10. Fighting to control the interview
11. Letting preconceived notions prevent you from hearing what is said

---

program *Fresh Air,* suggests that it is possible to remain respectful but still pursue your aims when interviewees (such as politicians and authority figures) begin to evade questions and give pre-programmed answers (2004). Listening to some of her interviews can be a great education in how to conduct respectful, but probing and insightful, interviews.

**Interview Data**

It is not enough to conduct an effective and engaging interview. As a researcher, you also have to convert that experience into data. In qualitative interviewing, a number of factors are involved in the creation of useful data. Some of those factors—the interview instrument, sampling, and creating records—exist in other research approaches, as well. Others are more a function of the qualitative interviewing approach, but even the factors that are found in other approaches take on a particular character in the qualitative interviewing approach.

In qualitative research, it is often said that "the researcher is the instrument." This phrase is intended to indicate that who the interviewer is and how that person behaves has a direct effect on the data that emerge from the interview. As Kvale points out, "Interviews obtained by different interviewers, using the same interview guide, may be different due to varying levels of sensitivity toward, and knowledge about, the topic of the interview" (1996, p. 35). But that is not the whole story. As is evident from the earlier discussion of the interview guide, in qualitative interviewing, the researcher prepares a guiding document. A qualitative interviewer also must utilize some way of recording the interview, probably involving some kind of audio recording device, and, for converting the recording into extensive notes, probably a transcription. The interviewer, the interview guide, the audio recording, and the transcription are all instruments in the qualitative interview approach.

There are no generally agreed upon standards for what qualities make for a good interviewer. Kvale (1996, p. 150), however, suggests, it helps if the interviewer is:

- knowledgeable
- organized
- clear
- gentle
- sensitive
- open
- purposeful
- critical
- possessed of a good memory
- able to interpret

I would add that an effective interviewer is aware of his/her preconceptions and cultural biases. I would also qualify a couple of the characteristics suggested by Kvale: An interviewer should be open, engaging in some self-disclosure, but not say too much; and he/she should be critical in the analytical sense (not naive), but certainly not judgmental.

As Rubin and Rubin (2005) have pointed out, how an interviewer handles his/her emotions can also have an impact on their effectiveness in qualitative interviewing. If you are tense, it will impair your ability to pay attention. If you act nervous, it will disturb the interviewee. You should anticipate making some mistakes and plan ways to facilitate your comfort with that and the other challenges you will face. Do not try to do too much. Show caring interest but do not be too intense. Recognize that empathizing can be taxing work.

The other side of the interviewing relationship is the interviewee. Whom you interview will depend upon the purpose of the study and the topics to be included. Since you probably will not be able to interview everyone you might want to, you will likely need to make choices about how to obtain an appropriate sample. There are three kinds of sampling that are often utilized in qualitative interviewing: purposive, snowball, and convenience. In purposive sampling, a researcher selects interviewees in order to obtain specific perspectives. Therefore, you would not want to obtain a random sample, the preferred way of sampling in statistical research. In qualitative interviewing, you may want to interview experts, exemplars, representatives, and/or witnesses. **Baker-Boosamra, Guevara, and Balfour** interviewed eleven stakeholders with at least three years' experience in the service-learning program (p. 486). **Okamoto** also sought interviewees who had expertise based on experience (p. 9). You may seek typical perspectives and/or atypical perspectives. The atypical perspectives may be important because they are conceptually significant; or it may be that obtaining marginal perspectives will help in the interpretation of more typical ones. You may also simply be seeking to maximize the range of perspectives included among your interviewees. **Okamoto** sought a varied cross-section of interviewees (p. 9).

Snowball sampling is iterative—the latter interviews are done with people recommended by earlier interviewees. You start with a small number of interviewees (probably identified purposefully) and build your list of potential interviewees through conversations with the initial sample. As Weiss points out, one problem with this technique is that it "will always underrepresent those who have few social contacts" (1994, p. 29). Snowball sampling can be done purposefully, or it may be utilized to develop a convenience sample.

In convenience sampling, you accept as interviewees almost anyone you can easily get to agree to participate. It is neither random nor purposive. It may be efficient, but because it can serve neither a statistical purpose nor a theoretical one, it is the weakest way of sampling and is not recommended.

Another possibility is that you may want to spend some extra time organizing a panel of interviewees, not just a sample. According to Weiss, "The idea in a panel of informants is to include as respondents the people who together can provide the information the study requires" (1994, p. 18). One way to organize a panel that is often used in qualitative research is the focus group technique. (For more on focus groups, I recommend D.L. Morgan [1993 and 1997] and B.L. Berg [2004].) If the central organizing element of the study is an event, you may want a variety of perspectives from people who were witnesses or participants. If you are studying an organization, you may want perspectives from different, well-defined roles. You may also want a panel of interviewees from a community, a network of associates, residents of a neighborhood, or a social institution.

Such sampling may be accomplished in a number of ways. You might place an advertisement—"seeking volunteers," or something to that effect—in an appropriate location, newsletter, or newspaper. You might visit a location where appropriate potential interviewees are likely to be found. Sometimes you gain access to interviewees through groups, associations, agencies, or institutions.

At the risk of stating the obvious, the interviewer and the interviewees create the data during the interview, but the interview and the data remain ephemeral if no records are created. It is important in research to create records that are reliable and accessible for analysis. In qualitative interviewing, creating records always involves taking notes and most often involves recording the interviews and turning those recordings into transcriptions for easier access when analyzing them. Relying entirely on the notes you can take may result in unfortunate gaps and/or inaccurate interpretations. Even if you are recording the interview, you need to take notes on what was said, how it was said, etc. Some of the nonverbal communication around the words said will be at least as important as the words. "Words alone are not sufficient for accurate interpretations" (D. Archer and R.M. Akert 1977, p. 449). Moreover, taking notes fosters more attentive listening, makes it easier (and more natural) to write down possible follow-up questions for later, and provides a backup in case the recording system fails. To improve the accuracy of your notes and enhance your familiarity with them, Rubin and Rubin recommend reading them over immediately after an interview and typing them promptly (2005, p. 111).

Transcriptions are crucial for creating reliable and accessible records of qualitative interviews. Two of the example articles specifically mention transcriptions (**Baker-Boosamra, Guevara, and Balfour**, and **Okamoto**), and the third (**Lyles and Mitroff**), because of its extensive use of direct quotations, appears to have used a transcription. Transcriptions do, however, come at some cost. The presence of recording equipment may constrain the interviewee, deterring candor. It also takes hours to transcribe an interview. Kvale says to allow five hours to type one hour of interview (1996, p. 169)—and that is just for the first draft. But recordings and transcripts are the best way to capture the language and phrasing of the interviewees, thus the best way to capture their perspectives for your research.

The interviewer is responsible for making a transcription possible—making sure the recording devices work (a backup recorder is recommended) and are set up to provide audible recordings for the transcriber. I recommend transcribing everything recorded. If the transcriptions are first drafted by someone other than the interviewer, the transcriber needs to be given clear instructions and the interviewer needs to review the transcript, listening to the recording while reading and editing the transcript as necessary. Even superb transcriptionists are not able to hear and transcribe everything accurately. People do not always talk in ways that readily translate into written form. Identifying the end of a sentence may be very challenging. Deciding where to note that there was a pause involves deciding when a silence is sufficiently long to be defined as a pause. When there is a silence that constitutes a pause, it is necessary also to decide to whom the pause belongs—the interviewee or the interviewer. If someone is speaking ironically, how do you know that? What is an ironic tone and how should that be noted in the transcripts? If someone laughs, it may be jovial or nervous laughter. How do you know which it is? The meaning you take from it will differ significantly depending on what kind of laughter it is. "Rather than being a simple task, transcription is itself an interpretive process" (Kvale 1996, p. 160).

Having prepared well for the interviews, conducted engaging and effective interviews, and created accurate and useful records of the interviews, your energies may now be focused on analyzing the interview data.

**Interview Analysis**

In qualitative interviewing, as in most qualitative research approaches, there is a sense in which the analytical aspect of the research is part of all that you do in the research project. Nonetheless, there is a portion of the qualitative interviewing research approach in which you focus more explicitly on analyzing the interviews you have conducted. That is the kind of analysis upon which this part of the chapter will focus.

Rubin and Rubin state that "data analysis is the process of moving from raw interviews to evidence-based interpretations that are the foundations for published reports" (2005, p. 201). Actually, you probably will focus more on your transcripts than the raw interviews during this part of the research project, but it is a good idea to return to the recordings of the interviews at key points to aid in your analysis.

Analysis has two phases—breaking the data down into codes and putting it back together in a way that presents the meaning(s) you have found. Weiss sees analysis as having four distinct processes: coding, sorting, local integration, and inclusive integration (1994, p. 154). In qualitative interview research, the purpose of analysis is not to generalize from the data, but to find meaning in the data. When they describe their methods of analysis, the authors of two of the example articles (**Baker-Boosamra, Guevara, and Balfour** and **Lyles and Mitroff**) speak of identifying "units" of meaning" or "units of analysis." Kvale sees this task as involving five steps:

1. reviewing the interview to get a sense of the whole,
2. identifying meaning units,
3. clearly stating the themes of each meaning unit,
4. interrogating the meaning units with regard to the purpose of the study, and
5. tying the themes together into a descriptive statement (1996, p. 194).

The themes that you derived from the literature are likely to be important in your analysis; those themes connect your interviews to your research questions and the research problem. You will use those themes and subtopics under those themes to begin classifying portions of your interviews. **Lyles and Mitroff**'s themes derived from the literature and the data. From the literature, they utilized inquiry systems borrowed from C.W. Churchman (1971) to see how well they could be used to describe the problem-formulation process. Three of their themes were addressed in Churchman's inquiry systems (credibility, commitment, and empirical support). In addition, their grounded theory approach allowed many other themes to emerge from the data—fear, political power, turnover, simultaneous crisis, human problems, problem avoidance, denial, and rigidity (p. 111).

**Okamoto** classified his data into three primary themes, which he called "nodes": "The purpose of interagency collaboration, the elements contributing to successful interagency collaboration, and the elements that negatively impacted interagency collaborations" (p. 10). The purpose of collaboration was to enlist the aid of experts who had different skills and access to different resources. Communication and cooperation were important aspects of successful collaboration. In addition to the absence of communication and cooperation, **Okamoto** identified passing the buck, blaming, withholding information, covering up, and premature termination of collaborative arrangements as elements negatively impacting collaboration. Under the subtheme related to elements working against agency collaboration, agency fear emerged from the data as worthy of special attention (pp. 12–13). He further broke the concept of fear down into such categories as fear of negative ramifications, fear of other agencies, fear related to physical safety, and fear related to financial liability.

**Baker-Boosamra, Guevara, and Balfour** analyzed their data based on their three themes: "reasons for and benefits of participation, program criticism, and suggestions for improving the program" (p. 489). Again, an important subtheme under reasons for and benefits of participation emerged from the interviews—*solidarity*. For the Salvadorans, solidarity was the primary reason for participation. To them it involved trust and a sense that they had international awareness and support. Solidarity meant that they were not alone in their struggle for justice.

As you analyze your data, you will also probably return to the themes in the literature; however, as shown in the examples, you should remain open to themes emerging from the data. An exciting part of analyzing the data derives from coding the data by classifying portions of the interviews based on the themes they address, comparing them to each other, combining or grouping them, and seeking connections and patterns among them. Some of that data will probably address themes you expected, but some may not, so you need to be prepared to add thematic categories as necessary. Coding the transcripts may be done within the text or in the margins of the text, whichever works best for you in retrieving the portions of the transcripts that are related to each other so that you can repackage them, pulling them out of the order in which they appear in the transcripts and putting them into an order guided by your themes. Repackaging them should assist you in recognizing how they cohere and in interpreting what they mean. **Baker-Boosamra, Guevara, and**

**Balfour** described how they used colors to mark different themes and theme boards to repackage the units (p. 489).

Repackaging the coded portions of the transcripts is a task that facilitates the synthesis involved in analysis, putting the data back together in a way that is guided by the themes you have identified and seeing how they connect to each other. It is in this synthesis process that you begin to build the data's coherence in terms of what it means for your research question. **Okamoto**'s Figure 1 on the causes and outcomes of agency fear demonstrates one way to repackage the meaning units in a manner that not only regroups the units but also meaningfully connects subthemes to each other. Absent the causal connections, **Lyles and Mitroff**'s figure on emergent themes (p. 111) represents a similar repackaging.

**Lyles and Mitroff** did both quantitative and qualitative analysis of their data. In this context I will focus on their qualitative analysis. In their grounded theory approach, they utilized categories based on the literature as well as categories that emerged from the data. Analyzing the interviews was based more on the "centrality and importance" of the themes, than on their frequency (p. 110). In qualitative research, coding themes is not simply a matter of tracking (or counting) specific words. As Weiss has pointed out, "Coding is thinking about the material" (1994, p. 156). Utilizing just two of the examples in **Lyles and Mitroff** (*turnover* and *credibility*) we can obtain a better sense of what this means. They coded a transcript section as addressing the concept of turnover whether the specific word (or words) used referenced retirement, promotion, or some other situation that led to a change in the organizational players involved in the problem-formulation process. The concept of credibility was also one whose presence had to be detected by more intelligent consideration than tracking specific words. The meaning of a sentence or a story might address *credibility* without ever including that term. One sentence that they coded as addressing credibility included the phrase "because I don't lie and am outspoken" (p. 111), but it did not contain any variation of the word *credible*.

Like **Lyles and Mitroff**, in his coding **Okamoto** did not rely simply upon tracking the appearance of specific words; he looked for the meaning of phrases, sentences, paragraphs, stories, etc. For example, in one section that he coded as "purpose of collaboration" the key phrase is "there are things I can't do" (p. 10). He categorized a quote that began "I think sharing information is real important" (p. 11) under the subtheme of "communication"—an aspect of the theme "elements of successful collaboration." In his section on elements of negative collaborations, he explained that the term *agency fear* came from one of his interviewees, but he came to see that subtheme as very important for understanding negative collaborations.

**Baker-Boosamra, Guevara, and Balfour** conducted their interviews in Spanish, but they used transcriptions translated into English for their analysis. Clearly, their identification of themes also was not simply identification of words used by their interviewees. For example, their interviewees spoke of *intercambio,* which they translated as "cultural exchange." One sentence that was coded into this category was "This program permits a mutual exchange of ideas and experience" (p. 491). As was mentioned earlier, the theme that they considered most important was identified because their interviewees frequently used the term *solidaridad,* which they translated as "solidarity" (p. 490). It emerged from the data in many ways and included such subthemes as awareness, trust, and support.

Through coding and repackaging the data you begin to clarify its meaning and improve your understanding. In composing the manuscript, your focus moves to sharing your understanding with others.

## Composing the Manuscript

The composition of your qualitative interview-based manuscript is, of course, framed significantly by your analysis of the interviews. It is also based upon your research problem and literature review work. But all of that needs to be put into an order and a style that works for your audience. Rubin and Rubin (2005, pp. 246–47) suggest four questions that you should think about when composing a manuscript:

1. What is the core idea or set of ideas that you want to communicate?
2. Who is the audience you are trying to reach in your writings?
3. What outlets are available to disseminate your findings?
4. What style and form of writing best communicates the central ideas in the outlets that will reach the intended audience?

In writing a manuscript, you are attempting to share as much of what you did and what you learned with your audience as you can, recognizing that they will never be able to understand your research the same way you do. You will have spent months working on improving your understanding; your readers will, at most, spend a matter of hours on it. Accepting this difference in your relationship with the research and theirs, your task is to facilitate a significant improvement in their understanding. You have two fundamental vehicles through which that task can be accomplished: the organization of your manuscript and the style of your writing. A traditional organizational format for academic journal articles is: introduction, literature review, methods, findings, and conclusion. **Okamoto** follows this format with one slight variation—the conclusion is titled, "Implications for Practice." **Lyles and Mitroff** use this same basic structure, but they do not always label the sections so obviously, and they add numerous subsections.

In the introduction, you discuss the general topic, your research purpose, and your research question(s). You begin by describing the general topic and explaining what makes it of interest to the field of public administration. Then you explain why your portion of the general topic is important, useful, and/or relevant to some public administration audience. Being fairly specific about who constitutes the audience you are addressing will help sharpen your writing. **Baker-Boosamra, Guevara, and Balfour** begin their article with an introduction to service learning that incorporates a literature review. Probably the most unique portion of their introductory section, though, is their brief description of El Salvador. This section provides evidence that the structure of the manuscript sometimes needs to be adjusted to better fit the content of the article.

The literature review explains how previously published research relates to your focus on the topic and is framed by the relationship of those earlier works to your research project. In the literature review, you refer only to those publications that explain what the field knows that relates to your research. It is not simply a compilation of brief reports about what the publications said; instead, it weaves reviews of the relevant literature together into a coherent argument about or explanation of what the field already knows about your research problem. It should (1) make clear how each citation mentioned relates to your research; (2) limit the treatment of each publication referenced to the aspects of that publication that are related to your research problem; and (3) include an internal summary at the end, highlighting the main points you want your audience to understand prior to reading about your research.

In the methods section describe your research approach in sufficient detail to provide the reader with an understanding of what you did and why you did it that way. Why was qualitative interviewing a reasonable approach to use? What was the general structure of your interview guide? How were the interviewees selected? In general, who were they (probably stated in a manner that protects their confidentiality), and why were they properly selected to pursue your research purpose? How and where were the interviews conducted? Why? How were the interviews recorded? If they were electronically recorded, how were they transcribed? What did you do to code and analyze the data? Were there any steps taken to deal with issues of bias and/or disputable interpretations?

The findings section is where you present the substantive results of your analysis. What do you consider the main understandings that can be taken from your research? How do you interpret the interviews, and what evidence can you present that those interpretations are reasonable ones? Can you suggest other interpretations and explain why you did not think they were the best ones? Even within a traditional organizational composition format, it is in this section that you have a number of stylistic decisions to make. (I will return to this topic shortly.)

In the conclusion you review the overall implications of your research, tying it back to the literature review, summarizing your interpretations, and making suggestions for further research. The only new material in this section should be the suggestions for further research. Other than that, the conclusion should be a section where you restate in a more general fashion the material that has been presented in the earlier sections of the manuscript.

Your writing style should be tailored to your audience. The words you choose must communicate your ideas precisely, express your voice clearly, and present your data effectively; in qualitative interview research, pursuit of this last goal is likely to include the use of direct quotes from your interviews. Public administration audiences appear to be more open to fairly traditional writing styles. Consequently, you may need to tone down the expression of your voice in order to maximize your audience.

However, you do have many stylistic choices to make about how to present the voices of your interviewees and your interpretations of them. Kvale, for example, has distinguished five general formats for presenting interview research findings: simple interview, dialogue, case history, narrative, and metaphor (1996, pp. 271–75). The first two present quotations in essentially the same order as they are found in the transcript. The third and fourth recompose the interviews into individualized stories. The metaphor format attempts to capture a key idea, but it takes a very high level of writing skill to use it effectively. Another common format found in public administration journals is the organization of quotations under the themes and subthemes utilized in the analysis of the research. All three of the articles used as examples throughout this chapter employed this last format.

Whatever format you utilize, your presentation of material from the interviews should reflect the voices of your interviewees. That means you will need to utilize an approach that keeps the perspectives and speech patterns of your interviewees at its heart. **Baker-Boosamra, Guevara, and Balfour** actually titled the section of their article in which they present their findings "Salvadoran Voices . . ." (p. 490). In almost every paragraph they utilized quotes from the interviewees to illustrate the points that they were making. **Lyles and Mitroff** tended to provide longer passages framing their themes and subthemes, and then presented quotations from interviewees to support their interpretations. Similarly, **Okamoto** utilized quotations from interviewees to provide evidence and/or examples related to themes and subthemes.

You may present quotations first, followed by your interpretations, or vice versa; but the quotes do not speak fully for themselves, so explaining what meaning you think a quote carries is necessary. For example, **Okamoto** introduced one quote by explaining its connection to his theme related to agency fear: "This fear is exacerbated by the language used to describe high-risk gang youth" (p. 13). Similarly, **Lyles and Mitroff** introduced different impacts of commitment on organizational problem formulation with the following explanations: "60 percent of the sample said that commitment to a particular view had a positive effect," and "Commitment is also viewed negatively when a high level of emotion was involved" (p. 112).

Certainly, when incorporating interviewee quotations into your manuscript, you should not simply list a series of quotations. Moreover, there should be a balance between your use of interviewee quotes and your original writing. "When interview quotes come from several subjects, each with their particular style of expression, many quotes with few connecting comments and interpretations can appear chaotic and produce a linguistic flicker" (Kvale 1996, p. 266).

Because a central purpose in conducting qualitative interviews is to share the perspectives of the interviewees, and because those perspectives are most authentically presented in the voices of the interviewees, I recommend minimalism in editing the style and quality of those voices. As Janice Morse and Lyn Richards have pointed out, "The goal of editing quotations is to maintain and convey the original expression" (2002, p. 186). Among the three example articles, **Okamoto**'s provides the best illustration of how to do this. Two quotes that he used may help to clarify what I mean:

> I want to take him back, [but] my staff would lynch me if I took him back [nervous laugh]. (p. 13)
> and
> So, when you read the report, you say, "[Gasp!] this kid is violent!" (p. 13)

Both of these quotes not only directly address the theme to which they are connected, but they also capture the interviewee's style of communication, including the nonverbals.

You want to share your interviewees' voices, but not in a way that reveals their identities. Remember your promise of confidentiality and edit to make sure that interviewees are not identifiable by aspects of their quotes. It may be necessary to provide context for the quotes as well as interpretation of them, but not in a way that identifies interviewees who have been assured that you will protect their confidentiality. It should be sufficient to provide information about the kind of interviewees from whom the quotations come (e.g., experts, exemplars, representatives, and/ or witnesses; typical perspective or atypical perspective).

Finally, because qualitative interviewing does not result in data that is easily summarized in tables, charts, and graphs, you will also face the challenge of not allowing the manuscript to become so long that it demands too much of your readers. Prune the quotes judiciously, asking yourself questions such as, "Is this phrase really necessary?" In asking such questions as you compose, edit, and recompose your manuscript, you will not only enhance your audience's understanding but also your own.

## Conclusion

Because public administration involves working with and for others and because those others have much to teach us about how to do our work better, qualitative interviewing is a valuable research approach for our field. It is a great way to gain insight into the perspectives of others.

All of the elements of qualitative interviewing work together to improve your understanding of the research problem. It takes more than a "semistructured" purposeful conversation with others to obtain a rich understanding of their point of view. A lot of advance preparation and careful development of an interview guide, including predetermined questions, potential probes, and follow-up questions, help to turn a purposeful conversation into a systematic research approach. Even with those aids, a qualitative interviewer still needs to pay careful attention and engage genuinely with those being interviewed in order to develop a partnership with them. Making sure that the interviews take place in a location that helps the interviewees feel comfortable and nurturing your relationships with them during and after the interviews are vital aspects of the project of learning from them. Effective qualitative interviewing entails building and maintaining a relationship. You cannot do it mechanically, but you do need to have a structure and a repertoire that facilitates genuine engagement. When you code, categorize, and analyze the interviews, you begin to reformat them to your research purposes, but if you want the research to present what you have learned from others, you need to keep in mind how they might see your work. A genuine engagement and relationship with them will assist in that effort. In more subtle ways, it will also assist in composing your research report in a manner that shares their point of view with your audience.

As you will see in the following chapters, because it is such a fundamental way of learning from others, qualitative interviewing can also be part of a larger research strategy, part of an ethnographic approach or a case study. But first, in the next chapter, we turn to an important variation on qualitative interviewing, narrative inquiry.

**Note**

1. Some people consider qualitative interviewing a data collection technique, not a research approach. I think that misconceives the centrality of interviewing in establishing the engaged relationship that is at the heart of qualitative research. In qualitative interviewing, data is not simply "collected," it is generated through the dynamics of the relationships among the researcher(s) and the interviewee(s).

## Exercises

1. Find an article in a recent (published in the last five years) professional journal that says it is based on semistructured interviews. Write a list of explanations (at least three) for why you think it fits the approach described in this chapter (or does not, if it claims to be and you disagree).
2. Imagine a research project that you think might utilize qualitative interviewing. Using Box 2.2, explain how your imagined project fits the criteria for when to use qualitative interviewing.
3. Imagine a qualitative interviewing research project that would benefit by being done by **you**. Using Kvale's list of desirable traits of a qualitative interviewer, what attitudes, skills, abilities, and other qualities make you an appropriate person to undertake this project?
4. Develop your interviewing skills by designing a short (10–15 minute) interview. Conduct the interview. Ask the interviewee to evaluate your performance. Evaluate your own performance against the criteria found in Boxes 2.3, 2.4, 2.7, and 2.10. Repeat this exercise several times.
5. Record one of the interviews done in Exercise #3 and transcribe it.
6. Code the transcript developed for Exercise #4.
7. Organize the codes created in Exercise #4 into at least two levels of generality (theme and subtheme).

## Recommended Readings

Berg, B.L. 2004. *Qualitative Research Methods for the Social Sciences*. 5th ed. Boston: Pearson Education.
Kvale, S. 1996. *InterViews: An Introduction to Qualitative Research Interviewing*. Thousand Oaks, CA: Sage Publications.
Rubin, H.J., and I.S. Rubin. 2005. *Qualitative Interviewing: The Art of Hearing Data*. 2d ed. Thousand Oaks, CA: Sage Publications.
Weiss, R.S. 1994. *Learning from Strangers: The Art and Method of Qualitative Interview Studies*. New York: The Free Press.

## Recommended Web Sites/Software

The Qualitative Report: An Online Journal Dedicated to Qualitative Research. http://www.nova.edu/ssss/QR/index.html.

Computer Assisted Qualitative Data AnalysiS (CAQDAS) Network. http://caqdas. soc.surrey.ac.uk/.

## Additional Journal Article Examples of Qualitative Interview Approaches

Lens, V. 2007. Administrative justice in public welfare bureaucracies: When citizens (don't) complain. *Administration & Society*, 39(3): 382–408.
Smith, Steven Rathgeb, and Michael R. Sosen. 2001. The varieties of faith-related agencies. *Public Administration Review*, 61(6): 651–70.
Teaster, Pamela B. 2003. When the state takes over a life: The public guardian as public administrator. *Public Administration Review*, 63(4): 396–404.
Van Slyke, David M. 2003. The mythology of privatization in contracting for social services. *Public Administration Review*, 63(3): 296–315.

## References

Archer, D., and R.M. Akert. 1977. Words and everything else: Verbal and nonverbal cues in social interpretation. *Journal of Personality and Social Psychiatry*, 35: 443–49.
Beebe, J. 2001. *Rapid Assessment Process: An Introduction*. New York: AltaMira Press.
Berg, B.L. 2004. *Qualitative Research Methods for the Social Sciences.* 5th ed. Boston: Pearson Education.
Churchman, C.W. 1971. *Design of Inquiring Systems*. New York: Basic Books.
Connell, R. 2006. Glass ceilings or gendered institutions? Mapping the gender regimes of public sector worksites. *Public Administration Review*, 66(6): 837–49.
Denzin, N.K., and Y.S. Lincoln, eds. 2000. *Handbook of Qualitative Research*. 2d ed. Thousand Oaks, CA: Sage Publications.
———. 2003. *Collecting and Interpreting Qualitative Materials*. 2d ed. Thousand Oaks, CA: Sage Publications.
Douglas, J.D. 1985. *Creative Interviewing*. Beverly Hills, CA: Sage Publications.
Fontana, A., and J.H. Frey. 2003. The interview: From structured questions to negotiated text. In *Collecting and Interpreting Qualitative Materials*, ed. N.K. Denzin and Y.S. Lincoln, 61–106. Thousand Oaks, CA: Sage Publications.
Goffman, E. 1967. *Interaction Ritual*. New York: Anchor Books.
Gross, T. 2004. *All I Did Was Ask*. New York: Hyperion.
Holstein, J.A., and J.F. Gubrium. 1995. *The Active Interview*. Thousand Oaks, CA: Sage Publications.
Kvale, S. 1996. *InterViews: An Introduction to Qualitative Research Interviewing*. Thousand Oaks, CA: Sage Publications.
Morgan, D.L., ed. 1993. *Successful Focus Groups: Advancing the State of the Art*. Newbury Park, CA: Sage Publications.
———. 1997. *Focus Groups as Qualitative Research*. 2d ed. Thousand Oaks, CA: Sage Publications.
Richards, Lyn, and Janice M. Morse. 2002. *README FIRST for a User's Guide to Qualitative Methods*. Thousand Oaks, CA: Sage Publications.

Richardson, L. 2000. Writing: A method of inquiry. In *Handbook of Qualitative Research,* ed. N.K. Denzin and Y.S. Lincoln, 923–48. Thousand Oaks, CA: Sage Publications.

Rossman, E.J. 1992. The use of semistructured interviews in developing Superfund community relations plans. *Sociological Practice Review,* 3(2): 102–8.

Rubin, H.J., and I.S. Rubin. 2005. *Qualitative Interviewing: The Art of Hearing Data.* 2d ed. Thousand Oaks, CA: Sage Publications.

Taussig, Jane E., and Ellen W. Freeman. 1988. The next best thing to being there: Conducting the clinical research interview by telephone. *American Journal of Orthropsychiatry,* 58(3): 418–27.

Weiss, R.S. 1994. *Learning from Strangers: The Art and Method of Qualitative Interview Studies.* New York: The Free Press.

# —3—

# Narrative Inquiry Approaches

In narrative inquiry, the researcher deliberately constructs interviews to obtain narratives or stories because of the special way that stories have of displaying the meanings of actions and events. Narrative inquiry, thus, is a special kind of qualitative interview approach in which the researcher seeks stories, not just extended responses. "What distinguishes narrative inquiry . . . is the focus on narrative and stories as they are told" (S. Ospina and J. Dodge 2005a, p. 145). As is the case generally in qualitative interviewing, a prime motivation for engaging in narrative inquiry research is to learn about something from a different point of view (or multiple "other" points of view). As Ospina and Dodge (2005a pp. 143–44) have explained, people use narrative inquiry to access "'local knowledges,' or aspects of experience that are unique to specific contexts and tell us something important about the human condition." Because narratives weave linkages among actors, events, decisions, actions, and results, they are a particularly valuable resource for understanding the meaning(s) of many kinds of life experiences, including experiences in public administration.

Although various forms of narrative analysis are used in policy analysis (F. Fischer 2003; E. Roe 1994; D.A. Stone 1988), organizational analysis (B. Czarniawska 1997), and planning (F. Fischer and J. Forester 1993), narrative inquiry has only recently become a topic of mainstream conversation in the field of public administration. In the early 1990s R. Hummel published two articles promoting the value of managers' stories in helping us better understand public administration (1990, 1991). David Farmer's 1995 book on the language of public administration was focused on public administration theory, not public administration research. R. Herzog and

---

**Box 3.1    Exemplar Articles**

Feldman, M.S., K. Sköldberg, R. Brown, and D. Horner. 2004. Making sense of stories: A rhetorical approach to narrative analysis. *Journal of Public Administration Research and Theory*, 14(2): 147–70. Available through Proquest.

Maynard-Moody, S., and M. Musheno. 2000. State agent or citizen agent: Two narratives of discretion. *Journal of Public Administration Research and Theory*, 10(2): 329–58. Available through Proquest.

Vickers, M.H. 2005. Illness, work and organization: Postmodern perspectives, antenarratives and chaos narratives for the reinstatement of voice. *Tamara: Journal of Critical Postmodern Organization Science*, 3(2): 74–88. Available through ProQuest.

---

R. Claunch published an article in 1997 using a mixed methods approach that addressed stories told by citizens and the ways that managers used those stories. In 1999 Jay White published a book on the narrative foundations of public administration research, but it did not address narrative inquiry as a research approach. S. Maynard-Moody and M. Musheno published a narrative inquiry article in 2000 (one of the exemplar articles in this chapter) and an award-winning book in 2003 that utilized narrative inquiry; however, it was not until 2005 that narrative inquiry was given concentrated attention as a public administration research approach in a mainstream journal; that year, *Public Administration Review* carried a three-part series on narrative inquiry (Dodge, Ospina, and E.G. Foldy 2005; Ospina and Dodge 2005a, 2005b).

In associated fields such as policy analysis, narrative analysis has often taken the form of what I call discourse or argument analysis (cf. Stone 1988; Roe 1994; Fischer 2003). That is not what this chapter will treat as narrative inquiry. In 2008 a ProQuest search for "public administration" and "narrative" resulted 212 hits, but many of the hits utilized discourse analysis (20) and/or were PhD dissertations (177). A few were historical or biographical, and several were book review essays. Only seven utilized narrative inquiry in the manner described in this chapter.

That so many were dissertations may bode well for narrative analysis as a research approach in the future, but many of those also used discourse or argument analysis, not a narrative inquiry approach.

As the work by Ospina and her colleagues demonstrates, narrative inquiry is used in applied research. The research upon which their 2005 three-part series in *Public Administration Review* was based was part of a program called Leadership for a Changing World (LCW). It was supported for seven years by the Ford Foundation, the Advocacy Institute, and the Research Center for Leadership in Action at Wagner/New York University (2005a, p. 155, note 1). The Web site for this program describes narrative inquiry as the core research approach utilized:

> We produce a leadership story on the work of each award recipient. The stories illuminate different aspects of leadership that awardees identify as central to their work and that may be of interest to other social change practitioners. This narrative inquiry is our core research component. (http://www.leadershipforchange.org/insights/research/narrative.php)

In addition to the individual stories, LCW produced a number of annual reports that present stories and describe commonalities among the award recipients on themes such as the role of visioning, integrating culture and values, and cultivating collaboration (S. Rao, M. Herr, and J. Minieri 2004).

In this chapter I first review the many possible meanings of "narrative inquiry" and "narrative analysis" and explain what definition serves as a platform for the descriptions, explanations, and guidance provided herein. Then I discuss why people use a narrative inquiry research approach. Following that is a section on design challenges that are specific to a narrative inquiry approach in qualitative interviewing. Because the logistical challenges are much the same as those described in Chapter 2, this chapter does not focus on them; instead, it focuses on data gathering and analysis in narrative inquiry. The chapter concludes with a section on writing narrative inquiry reports.

As was the case in Chapter 2, in this chapter I utilize three articles (see Box 3.1). The three exemplars, **Feldman et al., Maynard-Moody and Musheno,** and **Vickers**, show that narrative inquiry can be a valuable research approach for those interested in how public administrators view their work worlds.

## Defining the Narrative Inquiry Approach

*Narrative* is a term that has been given many meanings. Because of this, the label narrative is placed on a wide variety of approaches to research. Some people argue that most anything (any spoken or written presentation, films, videos, the architecture of buildings or landscapes, social phenomena) can be interpreted as a "text." Much of the research based on this rather inclusive definition derives from postmodern discourse theory, so I would call it discourse analysis, not narrative inquiry. Discourse analysis has been described as "distinguishable by its more strict focus on the content of talk than on its linguistic organization" (Schwandt 2001, p. 57).

One of the most inclusive definitions of narrative-based research in the field of public administration is implied in White (1999, p. 6): "All research is fundamentally a matter of storytelling or narration." Using that definition, all research is narrative research. Similarly, D. Balfour and W. Mesaros suggest that "the meaning of any human action, product, expression, or institution . . . can be treated as a text" (1994, p. 560). The implication of those statements is that most any research into public administration actions, products, expressions, and institutions can be considered narrative research. As was noted earlier, this complicates literature searches for narrative inquiry research in the field of public administration.

In identifying four forms of narrative in organization studies, Czarniawska (1998, pp. 13–14) provided a way out of this overly inclusive definitional landscape. She distinguished: 1) tales from the field—research written in narrative form; 2) tales of the field—stories collected from the organization; 3) interpretive approaches—seeing the organization as a story; and 4) literary critique—using literary forms to analyze an organization or organization story. Certainly there can be admixtures of these four types—e.g., literary forms or other abstract frameworks can be used to analyze tales of the field—but it is the second that points in the direction of what I am calling narrative inquiry. In my use of the term, narrative is a particular kind of discourse—a story that involves actors, events, and action organized by means of a plot that contributes to the story's contextual meaning. "A storied narrative is the linguistic form that preserves the complexity of human action with its interrelationships of temporal sequence, human motivation, chance happenings, and changing interpersonal and environmental contexts" (Polkinghorne

1995, p. 7). **Maynard-Moody and Musheno**'s use of narrative inquiry presents a good opportunity to clarify the distinction I am making. Their state agent narrative is derived from a discourse analysis of the public administration literature. Their citizen agent narrative is grounded in the stories they collected from cops, teachers, and counselors, i.e. is based on narrative inquiry.

Although narrative analysis may be applied to written documents— e.g., personal journals, autobiographies, biographies, memoirs—and oral statements from previously recorded material (see Chapter 5 for more on this), in this chapter I use the term narrative inquiry to indicate research involving collecting stories from others. Following J. Elliott's definition, those stories most often will "organize a sequence of events into a whole so that the significance of each event can be understood through its relation to that whole" (2005, p. 3). As Elliott has further suggested, the narratives will:

- contain (or imply) a clear sequential order
- connect events in a meaningful way
- be designed with attention to an audience
- offer insights into the topic or theme being researched

The more storylike (or, as Elliott called them, "fully formed") narratives include some orientation in time, place, and/or situation. There is also some complicating action, and its meaning is addressed. There may or may not be some resolution, result, or conclusion. Whether or not there is a resolution, the parts of the whole are linked through a plot. "Narrative knowledge is maintained in emplotted stories" (Polkinghorne 1995, p. 11).

Because plots (and meanings) involve interpretations, in most instances there may be more than one plot that could connect the parts of the story into a meaningful whole, leading to the possibility of different meanings being ascribed to the same collection of events and actions. This means that narrative inquiry should not be judged by whether the stories accurately report actions and events, but rather by whether they make available insight into meanings (ascribed or revealed). Sometimes researchers are explicit about not caring whether the stories they were told are true. For example, **Feldman et al.** said "Our concern is not with whether the argument is right or wrong or whether the events in question actually happened but, rather, with the understanding that the storyteller is expressing through the story" (p. 152). Similarly, **Maynard-Moody and Musheno** were more interested in the beliefs and norms of street-level workers than whether their stories were accurate. In contrasting the street-level citizen agent narrative found in their interviews with the state agent narrative that dominates the literature, they did not assert that the state agent narrative was wrong; instead, they concluded "each narrative highlights different aspects of the modern state" (p. 336). **Vickers** also explicitly recognized that "organizational life [is] a multiplicity, a plurality of stories and story interpretations" (p. 76).

Narrative inquiry, then, involves interpreting stories collected from others in a deliberate qualitative interview research approach designed to obtain stories for analysis.

## Why Narrative Inquiry?

Arguments for utilizing narrative inquiry research approaches generally address (1) the ways that they can improve understanding, and (2) the values and interests of the researcher. First among the arguments about improving understanding is the way a whole story gives meaning to its parts—and the way that the parts help give meaning to each other. The plot of a story is central to the way narrative gives meaning because it is through the plot that the story "relates events to each other by linking a prior choice or happening to a subsequent event" (Elliott 2005, p. 7). The linking of events, characters, etc., sometimes implies causality, but, more importantly, it imputes meaning. For example, if we hear about one person cutting another person, it is through the relationships among the characters that we understand whether the action is an attack or an act of surgery.

Czarniawska says that "in organizations, storytelling is the preferred sensemaking currency of human relationships" (1998, p. 385). One specific way that narrative inquiry fits for public administration research derives, then, from recognizing organizations and policy networks as communities of meaning (cf. Czarniawska 1998, p. 26). Organizational stories help us understand organizational relations and actions—and they help the organization to establish and maintain organizational culture and social norms, to organize the people who are part of an organization so that they may work toward a common goal and/or in a common style. Stories help us see organizational power. They also play a role in maintaining it and/or undermining it. Moreover, stories help us see the emotional life of organizations.

A second argument for using narrative inquiry relates to the way it incorporates temporality into our understanding of actions and events. As emplotted narratives, stories place events in relation to each other and in relation to an implied (or hoped for) future. The temporality is not necessarily as simple as chronological time. A plot is more than a sequence of events. It involves what Czarniawska has called *kairotic* time, "time punctuated by meaningful events" (2007, p. 387). The arc of a story often involves a complicating action, a climax, and a resolution— none of which would be recognizable if our only sense of them was as a sequence of events. Still, our understanding of chronological time influences our ability to make sense of stories. When stories are told in a nonchronological manner, it can be confusing to the audience. That is why films and novels often contain visual or linguistic markers to help the viewers or readers recognize when a segment is a flashback.

Their emplotted structure gives stories the ability to present causality (or at least perceived causality) and intentionality as part of the way that actions and events connote meaning—both for those telling the stories and for those hearing them. Thus, narrative inquiry also incorporates human agency, consciousness, subjectivity, purpose, and motivations. The main lesson of **Maynard-Moody and Musheno**'s research is about the different implications of the state agent and citizen agent narratives, but both of those narratives are based on human agency—the ability of people to act in ways that make a difference. In **Vickers,** the implications regarding human agency are double-edged. Her storytellers struggle to express their agency in a work world that is disinclined to acknowledge key aspects of their being.

This means that **Vickers**'s article also carries significance for the limitedness of human agency. It is not unusual for stories that incorporate human agency to also provide a way to address the limits that other factors (physical, spatial, cultural, social, relational, environmental, etc.) place on the potential for humans to author their own stories. Stories are "uniquely suited for displaying human existence as situated action" (Polkinghorne 1995, p. 5). **Maynard-Moody and Musheno**'s research could be said to imply that human institutions (including the administrative state) are limited in their ability to channel the human agency of their employees. Conversely, their research also shows the struggles that employees must endure to exercise their own agency within the limits that the institutions try to place upon them.

In addition to describing meaning in a valuable way, narrative inquiry also helps researchers further their personal and professional interests. Elliott (2005, p. 6) describes five reasons that the interests and values of researchers may incline them toward narrative research:

1. Interest in lived experience
2. Appreciation of the temporal nature of experience
3. Desire to empower research participants
4. Interest in identity and identity construction
5. Reflexiveness about being a researcher who is also a narrator

Temporality has already been addressed, but the other four add to the potential reasons for using a qualitative inquiry research approach.

Because narratives are well designed to elaborate on experiences that people have had, they are useful ways of accessing experiential knowledge, local knowledge that is grounded and textured. Ospina and Dodge have suggested that "narrative inquiry provides an internally consistent research approach . . . to capture complex interpretations of experience . . . [and] tap into [a] unique kind of knowledge" (2005a, p. 150). Similarly, D.J. Clandinin and F.M. Connelly (2000, p. 3) have recognized narratives as a way of accessing personal, practical knowledge. Narrative inquiry facilitates a multitextured engagement with practitioners. **Maynard-Moody and Musheno**'s article is an excellent example of that use of narrative inquiry. In addition, because of their ability to access and present personal perspectives, narratives are a fruitful way to highlight voices that have been excluded from mainstream considerations—marginalized people. **Vickers** is a particularly poignant example of the use of narrative inquiry for that purpose.

Often a researcher's motivation for engaging in narrative inquiry involves a desire to empower the storytellers by showing them that someone wants to hear their stories and by sharing those stories with a wider audience. It begins with a respect for the viewpoints of the storytellers, a valuing of them in their own terms (cf. Clandinin and J. Rosiek 2007, p. 50) and may derive from shared membership in a collective identity (cf. **Vickers**). Narrative inquirers recognize storytelling as "key in the transformation of experience into useful knowledge" (S. Stone-Mediatore 2003, p. 126).

One kind of knowledge that may be facilitated by narrative inquiry is self-knowledge. Narratives are useful ways of depicting both individual and group identity. Because identity is constructed in relation to time and others, stories are particularly helpful ways of constructing identity. We gain a better sense of who we are by examining the ways we change and the ways we remain the same over time. We also gain a better sense of who we are by examining how we relate to others and how they relate to us. This relational manner of better understanding identity also works for groups and institutions. It also may be helpful in better understanding the relationship that individuals have with the institutions for which they work; one way of framing the work of **Maynard-Moody and Musheno** is that it is a study of professional identity in which street-level public administrators are found to identify themselves as citizen agents, not state agents. **Vickers**'s article is about the way that individuals' relationships with others in their professional work settings affect their identity, their sense of being recognized and understood.

Narrative inquiry also has an impact on the self-knowledge of the researchers. Because narrative inquiry is a relational approach to research, reflexiveness (i.e., thoughtful reflection on the impacts of your actions on yourself and others) is an important aspect of it. Part of the need for reflexiveness derives from recognizing that the meanings ascribed to the stories are tentative and are not the only ones that could be ascribed. "Narrative inquirers work with an attitude of knowing that other possibilities, interpretations, and ways of explaining things are possible" (Clandinin and Rosiek 2007, p. 46). Narrative inquirers also recognize that their work becomes part of the lives of everyone involved, changing or adding to the meaning of their stories and their experiences.

Narrative inquiry, thus, pursues knowledge in a way that is different from other research approaches. Polkinghorne provides one way of understanding that difference by distinguishing paradigmatic (abstract and generalizable) knowledge from narrative knowledge, noting, "Whereas paradigmatic knowledge is focused on what is common among actions, narrative knowledge focuses on the particular and special characteristics of each action" (1995, p. 11). Instead of being generalizable to a larger population, narrative knowledge may be transferable from one circumstance to another. It is this transferability that led C.K. Riessman (2008, p. 3) to conclude: "A good narrative analysis prompts the reader to think beyond . . . [the specific story and] move toward a broader commentary."

Clearly, no single public administration research project can incorporate all of the things that narrative inquiry is capable of accomplishing. Each narrative inquiry research project, however, takes advantage of the ways that stories are used by people to give meaning to their lives

---

**Box 3.2   Reasons for Using a Narrative Inquiry Approach**

You want to:

- Use stories to interpret meaning
- Focus on lived experience
- Honor the meaning that actors give to their experiences
- Provide windows into different points of view
- Assist in giving voice to marginalized persons
- Incorporate temporality to help provide meaning
- Recognize human agency—choices, motivations
- Situate human actions within cultural, social, physical and environmental frameworks
- Explore organizational culture and power dynamics
- Access experiential, local, personal, practical, and transferable knowledge

---

and improves our understanding of those lives and the organizations, institutions, and dynamics of public administration.

## Design and Execution Challenges in Narrative Inquiry Research

Because narrative inquiry is a special form of qualitative interviewing, it shares many of the same challenges in design and execution. Having addressed these topics in Chapter 2, I will not belabor them here. Instead, I will quickly review them and then focus on those challenges that relate specifically to narrative inquiry. Issues relating to such research challenges as selecting interviewees, deciding where to conduct the interviews, and maintaining ethical and respectful relations with the interviewees are much the same. As in other qualitative interview research approaches, you need to clarify what you want to learn about and who might be in a position to help you gain better understanding. Being able to gain access and keeping your interviewees comfortable remain major considerations in deciding where to conduct the interviews. Obtaining informed consent, protecting interviewees' privacy, and generally doing

---

**Box 3.3   Design Challenges of Narrative Inquiry**

**Challenges shared with other qualitative interviewing approaches**

- selecting interviewees

- gaining access

- obtaining informed consent

- protecting privacy

- deciding where to conduct the interviews

- maintaining ethical and respectful relations with interviewees

- doing no harm

**Challenges specific to narrative inquiry**

- deciding whether to explicitly request stories

- if yes, deciding how much guidance to provide in the construction of stories

- if no, deciding how stories will be identified as parts of the responses given in the interviews

---

no harm to the interviewees remain central ethical concerns. You also need to nurture your relationships with interviewees and help them deal with post-interview anxieties.

Preparing for the narrative inquiry interview, because the approach requires obtaining stories, creates two new wrinkles: how to elicit stories, and how to identify the stories within the responses given in the interviews. If stories are explicitly requested, the design of the request may obviate the need to identify them; but if they are not explicitly requested, the researcher's definition of story and/or the type of story being sought may complicate the matter.

The three example articles utilized throughout this chapter provide some evidence relating to the common challenges as well as the new wrinkles. **Feldman et al.** selected interviewees from two city administrations that were going through organizational change (Charlotte, North Carolina, and Grand Rapids, Michigan). Access was gained by making initial contacts with top managers and executives. Their interest was in "how the administrations were undergoing new change regimes" (p. 150), so they interviewed people involved in those organizational change efforts—top level managers, mid-level managers, a union president, and others active in the transformation processes. **Vickers** wanted to give voice to a marginalized group in the workplace—people with invisible chronic illnesses—so she conducted numerous in-depth interviews with people who had unseen chronic illnesses, including at least five women and one man; her interviewees included people who had multiple sclerosis, chronic fatigue syndrome, cancer, leukemia, or glaucoma. Because **Maynard-Moody and Musheno** were interested in how street-level administrators used their discretion, they interviewed "street-level workers in five sites—two police departments, two vocational rehabilitation agencies, and one middle school" (p. 336). They chose to interview police, vocational rehabilitation counselors, and teachers in order to strengthen the foundation of their generalizations about street-level workers (Maynard-Moody and Musheno 2003, p. 167).* They did not want to learn only about police work, or counseling, or teaching, but about street-level public administration. Like **Feldman et al.**, they gained access by beginning at the top of the chain of command and working their way down, obtaining the needed permissions at each level, and concluding by getting work team permission prior to asking individuals for written consent to be interviewed (Maynard-Moody and Musheno 2003, pp. 167–69).

Privacy and location may be related issues. We learn from publications other than the exemplar article that **Maynard-Moody and Musheno** went to some effort to ensure privacy (2003, p. 170). The meetings were scheduled at the convenience of the storytellers—at the work sites, between classes or appointments, or while on patrol during a ride along in the down times between calls (2006, pp. 325–26). I cannot discern where **Feldman et al.** and **Vickers** conducted their interviews.

None of the example articles describes what the researchers did, if

---

*Maynard-Moody and Musheno also have two other publications based on the same research as that in the exemplar article: a book titled *Cops, Teachers, Counselors: Stories from the Front Lines of Public Service* (2003), and a chapter in D. Yanow and P. Schwartz-Shea's *Interpretation and Method: Empirical Research Methods and the Interpretive Turn* (2006). I utilize these sources to complement the information found in the exemplar article.

anything, to help their interviewees deal with post-interview anxieties. **Vickers** appears to have had the most personal relationships with her interviewees and would probably have had more contact with them after gathering their stories. Her personal concern about them and their anxieties likely resulted in efforts to make sure the interview process itself did not add to the complications in their lives.

There was much variety in the way that the researchers connected to the example articles prepared for and conducted their interviews. **Feldman et al.** interviewed administrators about how their organizations were implementing change, but did not explicitly request stories. They assumed that stories would "naturally emerge" and that they would be able to identify them. Using as a defining characteristic of stories that they "illustrate through specific example" (p. 153), they gave a research assistant a couple of examples of stories found in the interviews and then tasked that person with finding other stories in the interviews. The main challenge they reported was distinguishing a story from a description, so they "defined a description as a list without a plot" (2004, p. 153). A few times it was unclear whether they had identified one story or two, but that appears to have been settled by identifying the stories' themes to discern whether they had one story on one theme or linked stories that contained different themes.

It is not clear whether **Vickers** designed her research project explicitly to obtain stories. Because her article does not include traditional narratives and is a very personal style of narrative inquiry, it may have been inappropriate for her to do so. She presents "antenarratives"—fragmented, nonlinear, incoherent, unplotted stories. This approach was informed by her philosophy that her storytellers were "always in the middle of living their storied, non-linear, fragmented and polyphonic lives" (p. 76). Moreover, her preparation for and manner of interviewing was affected by her own "intimate knowledge and experience of the phenomenon under review" (p. 76); she has multiple sclerosis. For this reason, the stories she reports include some of her own. She referred to this as doing "hermeneutics from within the hermeneutic circle" (p. 77). That description provides evidence that even as a researcher she was aware that she was very much inside the phenomenon she was studying. She described her relationships with the interviewees as coproducing stories through successive encounters in which they influenced the construction of each other's stories.

On the other hand, **Maynard-Moody and Musheno** were quite

deliberate about seeking stories from their interviewees. At their first meeting with their interviewees, they explained and scheduled the story-collection process. They gave the interviewees a sketchbook with instructions and room to write text or notes on three stories; then they scheduled another interview about one month later to hear the stories. The instructions made clear that they wanted stories about how their interviewees' own beliefs helped them to make discretionary decisions. They also explained that the stories should have a plot, identify characters, describe the relationships among the characters, address their characters' feelings, and include contextual information about settings and circumstances (2003, pp. 169–70). When they met for the interview at which they would begin collecting stories, they "merely asked the street-level worker to tell his or her stories, which were tape recorded" (2003, p. 170). They minimized their interruptions during the telling of the stories, but followed up afterward to elicit information that would fill in gaps or provide more details. Typically, they met with their interviewees three times to hear stories and follow up on previously told stories.

These examples show that, as a form of qualitative interviewing, narrative inquiry is just as guided by purpose as other forms. It also is potentially limited by challenges such as gaining access, and its effectiveness is largely a function of whether trusting and respectful relationships can be developed. The key difference between narrative inquiry and other forms of qualitative interviewing is the need to obtain stories. As is clear from the examples, there is more than one way to successfully accomplish that task.

**Analyzing Stories**

There are many ways to analyze the stories collected in narrative inquiry. Riessman (2008) delineates four kinds of analysis: thematic, structural, dialogic/performance, and visual. Of those four kinds, two are more likely to be relevant for the field of public administration—thematic and structural. Thematic analysis categorizes the content of the stories based on themes the researcher is interested in. The object of interest is what was told, not the manner of telling. Structural analysis is also concerned with content but, in addition, attends to the form or structure of the narratives, usually to add a different kind of insight into the narratives. Those doing structural analysis may focus on a variety of structural aspects, from genre to story line to embedded segments or episodes. As

**Feldman et al.** demonstrate, it is also possible to utilize a rhetorical analysis technique (a version of a structural analysis). Whatever method is utilized to derive value from the narratives, it is important to work with aspects of the story form that distinguish it from other forms of discourse. "In narrative analysis we attempt to keep the 'story' intact for interpretive purposes" (Riessman 2008, p. 74).

Among the many methods for analyzing narratives, thematic analysis is the most common (Riessman 2008, p. 53). In thematic analysis, the contents of stories are examined by identifying stories that are relevant to the research purpose, categorizing specific content aspects (themes), and breaking down those aspects into subthemes. Regarding what themes and subthemes might be examined, there are unlimited possibilities. Two of the example articles clearly utilized some version of thematic analysis. **Maynard-Moody and Musheno** broadly categorized the narratives they referenced as state agent narratives or citizen agent narratives. State agent narratives depict street-level workers as agents of the administrative state, implementers who do their work with a focus on "carrying out the plans and policies of government agencies" (p. 337). In the counternarrative, the citizen agent narrative, street-level workers act within the context of rules, procedures, and policies of the administrative state, but their decisions "are case specific and guided by normative, rather than legal, ordering" (p. 347). Their decisions are improvisational, guided by judgments they make about the worthiness of specific clients; then they turn to the rules to find a way to implement their judgments. For the most part they view elected and upper-level agency officials "as irrelevant to their work" (p. 348). Within these general themes, **Maynard-Moody and Musheno** examined some more specific themes that gave meaning and importance to the state agent vs. citizen agent distinction. Within the citizen agent narrative, they addressed themes relating to the tension between serving the clients and the demands and limits of rules, the meaning of success, the role of moral judgments in decision making, and the importance of relationships over rules and pragmatism over authority.

**Vickers's** major themes were: 1) the unseen nature of some chronic illnesses, 2) inappropriate judgments of others, and 3) living with uncertainty. The invisibility theme seems to be the central one because the inappropriate judgments problem derives from it. When people cannot see evidence of an illness, they act as if it is nonexistent or minimize it, so the ill person feels unnoticed, misunderstood, and unfairly criticized. An example that she presented from an interview was:

> So, I went back to work after "chemo," full time, and everybody said, "Oh, you look really well." That's the hardest thing, because, okay, I look well but, you know, I am still pretty sick and I have got a life-threatening disease. (p. 80)

She also provided evidence of the uncertainty theme and addressed such subthemes as ambivalence, fear, vulnerability, futility, and impotence that derive from uncertainty. This theme connects to her description of the stories as chaos narratives, because in them life never gets better: "Every day you wake up and you live cancer basically, every day. You think, 'Oh dear. Oh, what's today going to be?'" (p. 81). The point of her analysis is to make the interpersonal dynamics visible and "to increase understanding and organizational justice" (p. 84).

**Feldman et al.** used a rhetorical analytical approach that placed a logical argumentation structure over the stories, making it a kind of structural analysis. Their analysis operated at three levels: 1) identifying the story lines, 2) identifying the oppositions, and 3) representing the arguments in the stories as syllogisms (in part to identify the enthymemes). Structural analysis is concerned with content but pays attention to narrative form—addressing the question, How are narratives organized? and focusing on *how* stories are told, not simply *what* is told (2008, p. 77). Because the article focuses on explaining their analytical approach, it is an especially rich example of the kind of thought that may be involved in analyzing narratives obtained through qualitative interviews. Their rhetorical analysis is an approach that "surfaces underlying logics and assumptions implicit in the story" (p. 151). To do that, they used the concepts of opposition and enthymeme.

**Feldman et al.** used opposition to find the meaning of a story element revealed by what that element is implicitly contrasted with. "When a storyteller describes a situation, one way to uncover meaning is by looking closely at what he or she is implying is its opposite" (p. 151). The most common oppositions they found included right/wrong reasons, political/nonpolitical reasons, and then/now. Another opposition that they reported is long term/short term. These oppositions may overlap quite a bit. For example, doing something for short-term gains and thereby losing long-term advantages is also doing something for the wrong reasons. It may also be doing something for political reasons.

**Feldman et al.** defined an enthymeme as "syllogisms in which one or more of the parts are not articulated or are probabilistic" (p. 155). To find those missing or probabilistic parts, they recast the stories told by their interviewees as syllogistic arguments, which are composed of major premises, minor premises, and conclusions. Most often they found that the major premise was missing. This was so because in everyday speech people often leave unspoken potentially controversial and/or taken for granted aspects of an argument. One example of an enthymeme that they reported is a storyteller's implicit premise that "creating a group identity and a mission will enable them to understand each other's perspectives" (p. 160). They point out that this premise leads to a very different argument than would a premise that creating a group identity results in "getting rid of differences in perspective" (p. 160).

After breaking down the stories into 800 syllogisms, **Feldman et al.** needed to synthesize an understanding of what they learned from the stories about organizational change. They used NUD*IST (Non-numerical Unstructured Data Indexing, Searching, and Theorizing) software to organize the data to help them identify the main themes about the roles of rule (structural) and mind-set (cultural) changes. Their rhetorical analysis revealed arguments embedded in the stories they collected that they say provided a deeper understanding than would have been possible had they restricted themselves to the explicit aspects of the stories (pp. 147 and 150). This is consistent with Riessman's position that "structural narrative analysis can generate insights that are missed when interpretation concentrates narrowly on 'what' is said" (2008, p. 100).

Another form of structural analysis that is frequently mentioned in the literature about narrative inquiry treats the stories as literary genres (romance, heroic tale, comedy, tragedy, satire, etc.). I could find no instance in which the literary genre mode has been utilized in public administration research; however, a variation of the literary genres mode, is found in Frank (1995). He has identified three categories of narratives: restitution, chaos, and quest. In the restitution narrative, the form is one where yesterday was good, today is problematic, but tomorrow will be good again. In the chaos narrative, life has taken a turn for the worse and there is no prospect that it will ever be better. Quest narratives hold chaos at bay by attempting to use the problem that is afflicting the protagonist to achieve some kind of improvement. Referencing Frank's work, **Vickers** identified the stories she shares as chaos narratives. Using another framework from Boje (2001), she also characterized them as "antenarratives"—"stories that are non-linear, incoherent and unplot-ted" (Vickers 2005, p. 76). Focusing on the protagonist's immediate experience, antenarratives tend to be non-linear and fragmented. Unlike other types of narratives, they have no result, conclusion, or resolution to facilitate the creation of a more coherent, holistic perspective. Given her purpose and her material, chaos narratives and antenarratives were good analytic frameworks for **Vickers** to use.

Whatever analytic method is utilized, a key distinction that has often been made concerning methods of analyzing stories is whether the method is a grounded theory approach or a theory-guided approach. In a grounded theory approach, the themes, categories, etc., derive more directly from the stories themselves. In a theory-guided approach, researchers place frameworks of their own making—or selected from the literature, or some admixture of those two—over the stories to interpret them. But the potential sources of theory are not so dichotomous. **Vickers**'s work might be described as grounded because of the importance she places on giving voice to her interviewees; but including her personal stories among those she reported, and identifying so closely with her interviewees, resulted in her being involved in the generation of theory in a way that complicates categorizing it as grounded. Her postmodernist standpoint may have been "helpful when interpreting stories replete with ambigu-ity, conflict, and discontinuity" (p. 75), but, except inasmuch as she is among the sources of the stories, it is not clear that this standpoint comes from her storytellers. And even though they described their analysis as "'grounded' in theory" (p. 165), the way that **Feldman et al.** placed rhetorical categories over the stories they collected is not a good example of the use of grounded theory.

It is clear that both **Vickers** and **Feldman et al.** would recognize these complications because both of them referenced the hermeneutic circle when describing their approaches (Vickers p. 77; Feldman et al. p. 167). The hermeneutic circle recognizes interdependence—our understanding comes from interactive relations, not unidirectional im-pacts. Theory doesn't *either* guide our understanding of the stories *or* derive from the stories; the theoretical concepts and the stories reflect on each other, and their synthesis informs our understanding. **Vickers** says that hermeneutics must always be done from within the circle and describes the "inescapable constituents of this . . . [as] background, pre-understanding, co-constitution, and interpretation" (p. 77). Recognizing the impact of her background and pre-understanding on her analytical

---

**Box 3.4    Key Analytic Choices to Make in Narrative Inquiry**

**Which analytic method to use**

- Thematic

- Structural

- Dialogic/performance

- Visual

- Rhetorical

**What kind of theory frame to use**

- Grounded theory

- Theory-driven

- Hermeneutic circle

---

framework, she would admit that the framework did not simply come from the interviews. Moreover, in citing "co-constitution" as a necessary aspect of hermeneutics, she implies that she, her interviewees, and their relationships are all involved in constituting the framework. **Feldman et al.** also referenced the double hermeneutic when they explained how they "moved away from the categories that the storytellers explicitly provided . . . to gain a deeper understanding of the change process" (p. 168).

**Maynard-Moody and Musheno** contrasted two theoretical frames, one grounded in the interviews (the citizen agent narrative) and the other deriving from the literature (the state agent narrative). So, their analytical frames derive from the stories *and* from the literature. It is the tension between those two views and its implication for the field of public administration that makes their research important. When the theoretical frame the professional literature uses to ascribe meaning to the actions of public administrators stands in such stark contrast to the theoretical frame the practitioners use in describing what they do, the field needs to re-examine its understanding of practice in a rather fundamental fashion.

The choices you make regarding your analytic method and your use of theory will do much toward structuring the way you present your work in a research text.

## Composing a Text and Re-presenting Stories

Clandinin and Connelly (2000) present four key concerns related to composing a research manuscript based on a narrative inquiry project: voice, signature, audience, and narrative form. The first three address issues related to the relationships involved in research. The tensions among those relationships complicate the task of composing narrative inquiry manuscripts. Voice refers to the issues of whether, how, and how much to try to include the voices of the research participants in the research text. The signature issue addresses that same set of questions with regard to the researcher's voice. Audience issues concern how best to communicate the research experience and results to others. As a public administration researcher who is trying to share with an audience the experiences of those who shared their stories, you are challenged to present the stories of individuals in a way that will interest an audience that has become comfortable with generalizations, abstractions, best practices, and/or transferable lessons. The particulars and nuances of the stories are what give life and rich meaning to them and are central to the value of narrative inquiry. Fortunately for those doing narrative inquiry, the field of public administration has a tradition of showing interest in case studies, another form of qualitative inquiry in which the particulars and nuances are key to the value of the research approach. (See Chapter 5.)

Narrative form issues relate to the shape and structure of the text in which the researcher attempts to manifest decisions made about voice, signature, and audience. How can the researcher as writer adopt a personal voice and retain credibility in a field like public administration which has traditionally valued the appearance of objectivity? The narrative form needs to present the research in a way that honors all three relationships— the personal relationships between the participants and the researcher, the integrity and professionalism of the researcher, and the professional relationship between the researcher and the audience.

Voice is a central issue for **Vickers**. Her article begins with these words: "The aim of this paper is to give voice to an 'invisible' and marginalized group in the workplace" (p. 74). She wants to help people with invisible illnesses become better understood by presenting their view of workplace dynamics. To give their voice a primary position in the article, she frequently quotes her interviewees. For example, quoting Beverly directly, **Vickers** writes: "If I say to them, 'Oh, I've got MS,' they say, 'Oh. You're kidding. Have you?'" (p. 79). Her description of

---

**Box 3.5    Key Compositional Choices**

- How to present the voices of your storytellers
- How much of your own signature to put on the text
- What audience to have in mind
- Which narrative form(s) to use
- How to mix narrative, description, and argumentation

---

the stories she reported as "antenarratives" provided further evidence of her recognition of their view. As was mentioned earlier, antenarratives are never complete because the "story tellers are always in the middle of living their storied, non-linear, fragmented and polyphonic lives" (p. 76). The "antenarrative" label honors her storytellers' views of their own lives as less than orderly and lacking a conclusion.

Signature is also a very important aspect of **Vickers**'s article. "My intimate knowledge and experience of the phenomenon under review, through having an unseen chronic illness, required me to find a . . . [philosophical] approach that enabled, even encouraged, my life experiences to be included in the research process" (p. 76). Instead of seeking to gain objectivity through holding her beliefs at bay (bracketing), she took an approach that required her to be aware of and transparent about her background, experiences, pre-understandings, and beliefs. Her first quotation was from her own reflections and included the statement, "A newcomer to this party would never know, judging by appearances alone, that any of us had any health problems" (p. 79). Introducing the first quote from her interviewees (Beverly, quoted above), she said that it confirmed her own experience. In "coproducing" the stories with her interviewees, she sought to present a multivoiced (polyphonic) telling of the stories.

Signature is not as important to **Maynard-Moody and Musheno**, but voice is. Although in the 2000 article, they do not directly address the issue of voice, they do in a 2006 chapter, describing it as a critical part of their approach (2006, p. 318). They also refer to their storytellers as "the experts on their own worlds," a statement that emphasizes the value of the storytellers' perspectives. Moreover, in the 2000 article, **Maynard-Moody and Musheno**'s interest in presenting the voices of their storytellers is evidenced in at least two ways: First, they open their article with two stories, thus placing the voices of their storytellers ahead of their own. Second, in explaining their choice to use narrative inquiry, they reference the texture, pungency, and vitality that stories provide and refer to stories as the "textual embodiments of the storytellers' . . . perspectives" (p. 336). Similarly, the first chapter of their book begins with three quotes from their storytellers, and they describe their research purpose as "to uncover their [street-level workers] judgments as they [the workers] see them" (2003, p. 25).

Because it is focused on presenting their analytical method, the **Feldman et al.** article does not directly address voice, but necessarily emphasizes the researchers' collective intellectual signature in the research—the "synthesis of [their] multiple perspectives" (p. 156). In order to "make the implicit explicit" (p. 157), their collective signature had to be given priority over the voices of their storytellers. This may have been more influenced by a judgment about what it would take to reach their audience than by the value they placed on the voices of their storytellers.

Identifying an audience is often a function of selecting a journal in which to seek publication. The three example articles come from two very different journals. **Vickers**'s article was published in *Tamara: Journal of Critical Postmodern Organization Science,* and the other two articles were published in the *Journal of Public Administration Research and Theory (JPART).* Although *Tamara* is clearly an appropriate journal for public administration scholarship, its readers are likely to be less mainstream than the readers of *JPART,* which is one of the most frequently cited journals in the field. *Tamara*'s audience tends to be receptive to critical theory and post-modernism, both of which are of interest to a limited portion of the public administration field. *JPART*'s audience tends to be interested in research methods. By publishing in *Tamara,* **Vickers** was reaching a smaller audience, but one that would quite likely be open to her approach. By publishing in *JPART,* **Maynard-Moody and Musheno** and **Feldman et al.** were addressing a larger audience but one that might need to be persuaded of the value of their narrative inquiry approach. This factor may explain why the **Feldman et al.** article so directly focuses on explaining their rhetorical analysis method. Nevertheless, both *JPART* articles provide evidence of the potential for reaching a large public administration audience while using a narrative inquiry approach. Moreover, the **Maynard-Moody and Musheno** research later resulted in a book that received a best book award from the research section of the American Society for Public Administration.

In addition to the considerations of voice, signature, and audience, a writer of a narrative inquiry research composition needs to consider the form of the composition. As I pointed out in Chapter 2, a traditional journal article format typically includes the following sections: an introduction; a literature review; the methods, setting, and researcher role; a description or presentation of data; the findings; and a conclusion. Even though the section headings reflect the specific content of her article, **Vickers** organized it along this traditional format. **Feldman et al.** utilized a similar structure but varied it somewhat to better present the logic and steps of their analytic method. **Maynard-Moody and Musheno**, as mentioned earlier, broke from the traditional format to highlight the stories of their interviewees. Clearly, many different formats can work when you are presenting narrative inquiry research (also see Box 3.6), but the question of how to incorporate stories is a crucial consideration.

Stories include characters, scenes, actions, and plot (sequencing of actions, often with a beginning, a middle, and an end). They are necessarily a more complex challenge to report than the data analyzed in many other quantitative or qualitative research approaches. Surveys can be presented by reporting summary statistics. Qualitative interviews can be presented using interview fragments. But narrative inquiry often involves some attempt to share and analyze stories in a way that reflects the people and their actions with some relation to the time sequences involved. This necessarily involves the researcher in re-presenting them so that they work in the new context of the research composition.

Because the stories are almost always collected in oral format, re-presenting them requires at least turning the oral stories into written ones. One of the fundamental challenges in re-presenting oral stories in written form is re-presenting the sound aspects (cadence, accent, pauses, inflections, etc.) of oral stories. M. Ely (2007, pp. 575–80) suggests a dramatic free verse poetry form of writing that can be used. She shows how line breaks can be used generally to indicate pauses, ellipses to stand for the kind of pause involved in groping for the next word, bold font to indicate increased volume, etc. The result is a composition that carries some potential for sharing not only the words in a story, but the voice of the storyteller. Below is an excerpt from one example that she shares (2007, p. 577):

So the midwife—she said
"Well touch him—he's yours!"

And so I leaned over
And I put my finger
And I touched his hand
And he tipped his head back
And he looked right up at me

It was just—it was just

Wondrous!

And I'll never forget, I'll never forget
I'll never forget that moment.

Chatman's (1990) three types of texts (narrative, description, and argument) help address other options involved in composing narrative inquiry texts. However, as Clandinin and Connelly have pointed out, in narrative inquiry research compositions it is not a question of which type of text to utilize, because narrative inquiry research compositions almost always contain all three (2000, p. 155). The issue, then, is how to mix the three types of text to best present your research. The three example articles utilized quite different, but very effective, approaches.

**Maynard-Moody and Musheno** begin by re-presenting two stories, one that they gathered from a police officer and one from a vocational rehabilitation counselor. It is after telling these stories that they include a fairly traditional introduction to the themes they derive from them and are going to examine in their article. In placing the stories at the beginning, they put the voices of their storytellers first—and they capture the power of the narrative form. Still, most of their article is composed of their description of the state agent and citizen agent themes (and subthemes) and their argument about what the tension between the two means for public administration. Placing the two stories first, they necessarily postponed the traditional introduction and literature review sections of a journal article, but these sections immediately follow the stories. The parts on the nature of street-level work, the two narratives, and the state agent narrative (plus its subthemes regarding discretion, self-interest, policymaking, and responses to discretion) contain the kind of material

---

**Box 3.6   Three Narrative Inquiry Manuscript Forms**

**Thematic Essay**

Introduction

Literature Review

Methods, Setting, and Researcher Role

Findings Presented in Explanatory or Argumentative
Fashion

Conclusion

**Narrative Story**

Opening story(ies)

Introduction

Literature Review

Methods, Setting, and Researcher Role

Additional Stories

Analysis of Themes

Conclusion

**Combining Thematic and Story Aspects**

Introduction

Literature Review

Methods, Setting, and Researcher Role

Narrative Segments and Themes

Patterns of Meaning Found

Summary/Conclusion

---

usually presented in sections labeled introduction and literature review. About halfway into the article they re-present two additional stories. The stories help make a transition from the literature-based state agent theme to the narrative inquiry–based citizen agent theme (plus its subthemes regarding discretionary attendance to rules, what it means to be successful in their work, how they rely on their own moral judgments in making decisions, and the importance of relationships and pragmatism in their work). **Maynard-Moody and Musheno** label their final section in the article a "comment," but it serves the function of a "conclusion," providing a summary description of the stories and reiterating the arguments made earlier about the disparity between the state agent narrative and the citizen agent narrative and what that means for public administration.

The stories that **Maynard-Moody and Musheno** re-present contain the major elements one expects to find in fully developed stories: characters, scenes, actions, and plots. For example, in Story 1 the characters include the assistant to the chief of police, a secretary, an African American female city employee, and a detective. Among the scenes included are the inside of the police department building, just outside of the assistant to the chief's office, on the stairs, and in the internal affairs office. Actions include the secretary asking the assistant to the chief for help, and the assistant to the chief introducing himself and conversing with the African American female before walking her up to the internal affairs office to introduce her to a detective there. The plot is embedded in the sequence of events showing how the assistant to the chief reacted to and assisted the African American female. The story also presents the emotions of some of the characters—the fear of the African American female and the shock of the assistant to the chief regarding her level of apprehension—elements often missing in other research approaches.

Because the **Vickers** article re-presents fragmented stories (or "antenarratives") they do not contain all of the common elements of stories. Despite this, the stories **Vickers** re-presents do contain characters, scenes, and actions. The characters include: Vickers; her husband, Michael; eight interviewees (Beverly, Linda, June, Dave, Shelley, Fred, Peter, and Rosalie); some medical professionals; and some unnamed children who have cancer. Scenes in the stories she represents include a dinner party, a radiotherapy clinic, and a few work settings. Actions include a confrontation between June and Dave, a conversation between **Vickers** and her neurologist, and various coping strategies—including both not telling people about their diseases, and trying to explain to others what their diseases do to them. Even without plots, the shared thoughts and dialogues still present the emotional drama of Vickers and her research partners. For example, June relates aspects of her relationship with a man who knows about her glaucoma but seems incapable of recognizing its import, which she finds irritating and annoying. The storytellers also discuss their frustration, fear, sadness, and anger.

As was stated earlier, **Vickers**'s article retains a rather traditional structure. The first section is introductory, explaining the purpose of and perspective involved in the article. It is followed by sections that review the literature, covering the value of stories and narratives and of a theoretical and methodological perspective that allowed her to incorporate her life experiences (not seek an objective perspective) as long as she was aware of her own prejudices. Next is a methods section. Her findings section is broken into themes regarding uncertainty, heterogeneity, fragmentation and difference, and misunderstanding. Finally, her conclusion addresses implications for organizational analysis and how she hopes to have contributed toward creating "a more just working environment" (p. 85). In addition to the fragmented stories, her article includes both description and argument. She describes the challenges involved in the lives of people with chronic, unseen illnesses, using her own experiences and those of her interviewees as evidence of her descriptive characterizations. Her arguments address such things as the value of narratives, of an openly subjective approach, and of a postmodern perspective for improving organizational justice.

The article by **Feldman et al.** is an argument for and a description of a particular approach to narrative inquiry. It begins with an introduction to the use of narrative inquiry by public administration and public policy scholars. It then explains the difference between stories and narratives: "A story is a subset of narrative" (p. 149). Next comes an argument for having some kind of analytical strategy, followed by an argument for the value of their rhetorical analysis method. The bulk of the article is a demonstration of their rhetorical analysis method that shows how it was used to examine four different stories. Prior to concluding, they include sections that focus on the coding and theory generation processes.

The stories in the **Feldman et al.** article provide the starting point for taking the reader step-by-step through their analytical method. The stories are re-presented, but they are quickly reframed into a "story line" that is the object of their rhetorical analysis. In recasting the stories as story lines, they move away from the traditional elements of the story (characters, scene, action, and plot), instead treating the stories as arguments, even recasting them further as syllogisms. In doing so, they lose some of the power commonly ascribed to stories, but they gain a new ability to identify and examine the argumentative meaning of the stories and the unstated and assumed elements of those arguments.

These three example articles provide evidence that there are many ways to organize a narrative inquiry research composition. Each has advantages and disadvantages. How you choose to organize your research composition should be a function of your interests as a researcher, your skills as a writer, the audience you are addressing, and your relationship with the storytellers.

## Conclusion

Narrative inquiry is a special form of qualitative interviewing. Collecting stories through interviews and analyzing them as stories that give meaning to actions, decisions, events, and results can be a valuable research approach for those interested in how others view their own experiences. Narrative inquiry researchers recognize the role that temporality, human agency, and relationships play in constructing meaning. People who do narrative inquiry are seeking meaning, not factual accuracy.

In addition to the challenges faced by all researchers engaged in qualitative interviewing, narrative inquirers must decide how to get stories, how to analyze them, and how to represent them. Struggling with those challenges is not easy but can result in unique contributions to knowledge enhancement in the field of public administration.

## Exercises

1. Imagine a research project that you think might be pursued using narrative inquiry research. Using Box 3.2, explain how your imagined project fits the criteria for when to use a narrative inquiry approach.
2. For that same research project, explain how directive you would be in eliciting stories and why. Would you be as directive as **Maynard-Moody and Musheno** or simply look for stories in your interviews as **Feldman et al.** did?
3. Identify what stories 2, 3, and 4 in the **Maynard-Moody and Musheno** article imply about human agency.
4. Identify what stories 2, 3, and 4 in the **Maynard-Moody and Musheno** article imply about the role time plays in affecting the meaning of a story.
5. Analyze the **Maynard-Moody and Musheno** article to identify what the stories add to our understanding of the issue they present. If some of the stories they collected were not re-presented, what would be missing? How do the stories add to the argument they are making?
6. Make an argument for or against doing a narrative inquiry

project where you are among the sources of the stories (as was **Vickers**).

7. Make an argument for or against the kind of rhetorical analysis utilized by **Feldman et al.**

8. Working from a) a recording of an interview or some other oral presentation, and b) a transcript of that same interview or presentation, construct a new transcript that uses a dramatic free verse format (as did Ely 2007). Do the transcripts carry different meanings? If so, explain. If not, explain why not.

## Recommended Readings

Clandinin, D.J. 2007. *Handbook of Narrative Inquiry: Mapping a Methodology.* Thousand Oaks, CA: Sage Publications.

Czarniawska, B. 1997. *Narrating the Organization: Dramas of Institutional Identity.* Chicago: University of Chicago Press.

Ely, M., R. Vinz, M. Downing, and M. Anzul. 1997. *On Writing Qualitative Research: Living by Words.* Bristol, PA: The Falmer Press.

Maynard-Moody, S., and M. Musheno. 2003. *Cops, Teachers, Counselors: Stories from the Front Lines of Public Service.* Ann Arbor: University of Michigan Press.

Stone-Mediatore, S. 2003. *Reading Across Borders: Storytelling and Knowledges of Resistance.* New York: Palgrave Macmillan.

Yanow, D., and P. Schwartz-Shea, eds. 2006. *Interpretation and Method: Empirical Research Methods and the Interpretive Turn.* Armonk, NY: M.E. Sharpe.

## Recommended Web Site

Leadership for a Changing World, Institute for Sustainable Communities. http://www.leadershipforchange.org/.

## References

Balfour, D., and W. Mesaros. 1994. Connecting local narratives: Public administration as a hermeneutic science. *Public Administration Review,* 54(6): 559–64.

Boje, D. M. 2001. *Narrative Methods for Organizational and Communication Research.* Thousand Oaks, CA: Sage Publications.

Chatman, S. 1990. *Coming to Terms: The Rhetoric of Narrative in Fiction and Film.* London: Cornell University Press.

Clandinin, D.J., and F.M. Connelly. 2000. *Narrative Inquiry: Experience and Story in Qualitative Research.* San Francisco, CA: Jossey-Bass.

Clandinin, D.J., and J. Rosiek. 2007. Mapping a landscape of narrative inquiry. In *Handbook of Narrative Inquiry: Mapping a Methodology,* ed. D.J. Clandinin, 35–75. Thousand Oaks, CA: Sage Publications.

Czarniawska, B. 1997. *Narrating the Organization: Dramas of Institutional Identity.* Chicago: University of Chicago Press.

———. 1998. *A narrative Approach in Organization Studies.* Thousand Oaks, CA: Sage Publications.

———. 2007. Narrative inquiry in and about organizations. In *Handbook of Narrative Inquiry,* D.J. Clandinin, ed., 383–404. Thousand Oaks, CA: Sage Publications.

Dodge, J., S.M. Ospina, and E.G. Foldy. 2005. Integrating rigor and relevance in public administration scholarship. *Public Administration Review,* 65(3): 286–300.

Elliott, J. 2005. *Using Narrative in Social Research: Qualitative and Quantitative Approaches.* Thousand Oaks, CA: Sage Publications.

Ely, M. 2007. In-forming re-presentations. In *Handbook of Narrative Inquiry,* ed. D.J. Clandinin, 567–98. Thousand Oaks, CA: Sage Publications.

Farmer, D.J. 1995. *The Language of Public Administration: Bureaucracy, Modernity, and Postmodernity.* Tuscaloosa: University of Alabama Press.

Fischer, F. 2003. *Reframing Public Policy: Discursive Politics and Deliberative Practices.* Oxford, UK: Oxford University Press.

Fischer, F., and J. Forester, eds. 1993. *The Argumentative Turn in Policy Analysis and Planning.* Durham, NC: Duke University Press.

Frank, A. W. 1995. *The Wounded Storyteller: Body, Illness and Ethics.* Chicago: University of Chicago Press.

Herzog, R., and R. Claunch. 1997. Stories citizens tell and how administrators use types of knowledge. *Public Administration Review,* 57(5): 374–79.

Hummel, R. 1990. Uncovering validity criteria for stories managers hear and tell. *American Review of Public Administration,* 20: 303–14.

———. 1991. Stories managers tell: Why they are as valid as science. *Public Administration Review,* 51: 31–41.

Maynard-Moody, S., and M. Musheno. 2003. *Cops, Teachers, Counselors: Stories from the Front Lines of Public Service.* Ann Arbor: University of Michigan Press.

———. 2006. Stories for research. In *Interpretation and Method: Empirical Research Methods and the Interpretive Turn,* ed. D. Yanow and P. Schwartz-Shea, 316–30. Armonk, NY: M.E. Sharpe.

Ospina, S., and J. Dodge. 2005a. It's about time: Catching method up to meaning—the usefulness of narrative inquiry in public administration research. *Public Administration Review,* 65(2): 143–57.

———. 2005b. Narrative inquiry and the search for connectedness: Practitioners and academics developing public administration scholarship. *Public Administration Review,* 65(4): 409–23.

Polkinghorne, D.E. 1995. Narrative configuration in qualitative analysis. In *Life History and Narrative,* ed. J. A. Hatch and R. Wiseniewski, 5–23. New York: Routledge Farmer.

Rao, S., M. Herr, and J. Minieri. 2004. Social change leadership from the inside: A group portrait of the 2004 Leadership for a Changing World awardees. Accessed August 12, 2008 from http://www.leadershipforchange.org/insights/research/files/Group4Portrait.pdf.

Riessman, C.K. 2008. *Narrative Methods for the Human Sciences.* Los Angeles: Sage Publications.

Roe, E. 1994. *Narrative Policy Analysis: Theory and Practice.* Durham, NC: Duke University Press.

Schwandt, Thomas A. 2001. *Dictionary of Qualitative Inquiry.* 2d ed. Thousand Oaks, CA: Sage Publications.

Stone, D.A. 1988. *Policy Paradox and Political Reason.* Glenview, IL: Scott, Foresman.

Stone-Mediatore, S. 2003. *Reading Across Borders: Storytelling and Knowledges of Resistance.* New York: Palgrave Macmillan.

White, J.D. 1999. *Taking Language Seriously: The Narrative Foundations of Public Administration Research.* Washington, DC: Georgetown University Press.

# −4−

# Ethnographic Approaches

Ethnographic research has much to offer to the field of public administration. Since public administration is an applied field, it is often concerned with issues regarding implementation of policies and programs. For us it is not enough to know what the policy says or what the mission of the program is; we need to know how the policy is implemented and how the program impacts those it is intended to impact. Ethnographic research, because it is done in the field and depends upon attentive observation, is well suited to assisting us in gaining a better understanding of what impacts programs have and what happens when policies are implemented.

Nonetheless, ethnographies are not frequently published in mainstream public administration journals; however, they are found in journals that public administration professionals read. Journals in which ethnographies are regularly published include *Human Organization, Journal of Contemporary Ethnography, Contemporary Sociology,* and *Current Anthropology.*

Because of the time and effort involved, traditional ethnographic research is more likely to be found in dissertations and books. A summer 2006 ProQuest search for "public administration" and "ethnography" resulted in a list that included 33 dissertations. Those dissertations were on topics such as homeland security, community policing, homeless policy administration, a federal housing program, managed health care, endangered species protection, the profession of program evaluation, implementation of the 1988 Anti-Drug Abuse Act, nonprofit organizations in Japan, and urban water utility reform in South India. Classic books in public administration that involve ethnographic research ap-

---

**Box 4.1   Exemplar Articles**

Heyman, J. McC. 1995. Putting power in the anthropology
of bureaucracy: The Immigration and Naturalization
Service at the Mexico-United States border. *Current
Anthropology*, 36(2): 261–87. Available through
EBSCOhost socINDEX with full text.

Heyman, J. McC. 2001. Class and classification at the U.S.-
Mexico border. *Human Organization*, 60(2): 128–40.
Available through ProQuest Research Library.

Heyman, J. McC. 2002. U.S. immigration officers of Mexican
ancestry as Mexican Americans, citizens, and
immigration police. *Current Anthropology*, 43(3): 479–
96. Available through EBSCOhost socINDEX with full
text.

*Note: Because in this chapter the exemplar articles were all written by
the same author, the conventions utilized in other chapters to highlight
their identification are not utilized.*

---

proaches include H. Kaufman's *The Forest Ranger* (1960/2006) and
M. Lipskey's *Street Level Bureaucracy: Dilemmas of the Individual
in Public Services* (1980).

Ethnographic work is also commissioned and published by government agencies. A 2003 U.S. General Accounting Office (GAO;
now the Government Accountability Office) study explored the use
of ethnographic research to inform the action of 10 federal agencies,
including such diverse agencies as the Bureau of the Census, the
National Marine Fisheries Service, the Centers for Disease Control
and Prevention, the National Park Service, and the Department of
Labor's Employment and Training Administration. The main utility
that GAO ascribed to ethnographic research was to assist in gaining
"a better understanding of the sociocultural life of a group whose beliefs and behavior were important to a federal program" (2003, p. 3),
but ethnographic studies have also been used to better understand the
internal behavioral dynamics of organizations—their organizational
cultures—or the relational dynamics between organizations and the
people they serve (or impact).

In this chapter I first discuss several definitions of the ethnographic approach and some of the wide variety of types of ethnography that have been identified. Following that is a section on the design challenges that are most frequently associated with doing ethnographic research. Next I address the logistical challenges ethnographic researchers typically face. Then there is a section on data gathering, which emphasizes how to do observational fieldwork and take field notes. The chapter concludes with sections on how to analyze ethnographic data and write up an ethnographic report.

Throughout the chapter I utilize several articles written by Josiah Heyman that are based on ethnographic research and address topics of interest to public administration professionals (see Box 4.1). Interested in developing an anthropology of bureaucracies because "bureaucracies are the preeminent technology of power in the contemporary world" (1995, p. 262), Heyman has studied U.S. immigration policy implementation by examining the work of officials in the Immigration and Naturalization Service (INS), specifically immigration officers working at the U.S.–Mexico border. His work provides insights into such issues as how classification practices affect class relations, how the work practices of immigration officers of Mexican ancestry affect their self images and the ways they relate to Mexicans attempting to immigrate into the United States, how bureaucratic work enacts organizational power, and how the INS contributes to the exploitation of immigrant laborers. More important for this textbook, his work models ethnographic research in many specific and exemplary ways.

**Defining the Ethnographic Approach**

There are, of course, some disputes about what constitutes an ethnographic approach, but there is a pretty good consensus regarding the basic definition. Things get a lot more complicated when people begin to distinguish types of ethnography.

Before defining the ethnographic approach, it might be helpful to point out that there are significant similarities between a case study approach (see Chapter 5) and an ethnographic approach. Ethnography is sometimes described as a kind of case study. M.D. LeCompte and J.J. Schensul, for example, say that "ethnographies are culturally informed case studies" (1999, p. 82). Heyman, the ethnographer whose work we will examine closely in this chapter, has also referred to his research approach using the term "case study" (e.g., Heyman 1995, p. 261). Aspects of an ethnographic approach that are often used to distinguish it from a case study approach include the degree to which ethnography tends to include open-ended interviews and participant observation. Whereas case studies may focus on an event or the making of a decision, ethnographies are typically focused on understanding some group and relying upon the concept of culture in understanding that group.

D.M. Fetterman defines ethnography as "the art and science of describing a group or culture" (1998, p. 1). He recognizes the creativity that may be involved in doing ethnographic work but suggests that the work is also scientific. Qualitative approaches to ethnographic research tend to emphasize the creative aspect, while quantitative approaches emphasize adherence to social science methods. The part of his definition that describes the focus of ethnographic work as a group or culture implies that there may be a significant range of population sizes among the potential objects of ethnographic research. Initially, ethnographic research was used mostly to describe the cultures of non-Western societies, but "ethnography is no longer a method used only to study foreign cultures; it has also become a method to study what is foreign or strange in our society and how social subcultures or subworlds are constructed—the adventure that begins just around the corner" (U. Flick 1999, p. 641). Some of those subcultures may even be formed in the relations between cultures, or in the organizations that are responsible for specific aspects of those relations.

According to J.W. Creswell, "An ethnography is a description and interpretation of a cultural or social group or system" (1998, p. 58). His definition adds to the descriptive aspect of ethnography a recognition of its interpretive aspect, thus distancing it a bit further from at least some definitions of science. Echoing the "group or culture" phrasing of Fetterman's definition, it also offers a simple, but wide-ranging delineation of what the ethnographic researcher studies. It may be a cultural group, social group, cultural system, or social system. None of these four categories has clear and clean boundaries, and it is not always easy to distinguish them from each other, but each of the four opens up additional possibilities about what might be studied using an ethnographic approach.

Defining ethnography as "the work of describing a culture [and suggesting that] the essential core of this activity aims to understand another way of life from the native point of view," Spradley attends more to the purpose of the research than its object (Berg 2004, p. 147). His definition highlights a fundamental feature of ethnography—its attempt to gain an emic understanding, an understanding from a native or insider's point of view. An ethnographer goes into the field in order to participate, observe, and talk with members of a culture or group to better understand their points of view and present them to an audience.

Finally, J. Van Maanen takes Spradley's contribution a bit further when he says the task of ethnography is "representing the social reality of others through the analysis of one's own experience in the world of these others" (1988, p. ix). Van Maanen's definition recognizes the gap between the social realities of others and the representation of those realities by an outsider who can only describe his or her perspective on their worlds. It also points by implication to another key aspect of ethnography—that it involves going into "the field" to study a *current* culture or group. In order for the ethnographer to experience the world of others, he or she needs to be able to become immersed in it as it happens. "Ethnography is distinguished by the collection of data by means of human observation and interaction in a local setting, with the researcher as the primary data collection tool" (GAO 2003, p. 6).

In sum, qualitative approaches to ethnographic research involve engaging in field study of a group or culture in order to interpretively describe it in a way that appreciates (and attempts to present it from) the viewpoints of members so that an outside audience can better understand the group or culture. These days, dealing with the plurality of viewpoints within a group or culture is also a key aspect of ethnographic research. "Ethnographers increasingly find themselves studying 'communities' that are defined as much by their conflicts, factions, and divisions as they are by their commonalities" (M. Angrosino and K.A. Mays de Pérez 2000, p. 680).

**Types of Ethnography**

The definition of ethnography has evolved as ethnographic research approaches have been applied to new subjects in creative ways. This has led to the identification of quite a variety of types of ethnography. Some of the more basic types include: traditional, applied, urban, medical, educational, administrative, and autoethnography. Traditional ethnography involves extended observation in a local setting and describes for a scholarly or academic audience an unfamiliar culture, usually in a foreign land, perhaps focusing on a specific village or set of villages. Applied ethnography may be done by academics, but in addition to describing a culture it aims to influence (or at least inform) policy or influence social change. Urban ethnography focuses on subcultures (e.g., drug users, homeless people, gays, lesbians, and bisexuals) found in the cities of Western societies. Medical, educational, and administrative ethnography seem to have obtained their labels based on the people doing or funding the ethnography (nurses or other medical professionals, educational professionals, or administrators or government officials), rather than the subcultures on which they may focus. Autoethnography attends more directly to the researcher's situation in doing ethnographic research, acknowledging the singularity and limitations of his or her personal perspective while using it to gain understanding of a culture that he or she entered into for the purpose of observing and writing about it.

The list of types of ethnography that have been delineated seems to grow almost every day, so I will not attempt to include them all. The types most obviously related to public administration are applied, urban, and (of course) administrative.

### Choosing an Ethnographic Approach

Public administration professionals who are interested in using an ethnographic research approach have choices to make about exactly what type of ethnography to do and how to proceed. Although there are many situations in which you might choose to do ethnographic research, three that seem particularly suitable for public administration are: (1) studying an organizational culture, (2) studying the relations of an organization with its clients or the people it impacts, and (3) studying the culture of a community being served or impacted by a program or policy in order to improve policies and/or their implementation. Heyman's work contributes toward understanding aspects of the INS's organizational culture and the relations between the INS and Mexican immigrants.[1]

Specific characteristics of the ethnographic approach may also help you to decide whether it is a good one for the research project you are considering. A checklist based on these characteristics is found in Box 4.2.

Using this checklist to analyze Heyman's research may help to clarify what the items mean. One of the signature aspects of ethnographic research is that it involves going on location and doing fieldwork— observing, listening, conversing, and otherwise engaging people directly.

---

**Box 4.2    Reasons for Using a Qualitative Ethnographic Approach**

- To study a phenomenon through fieldwork on location in its natural setting
- To use the concept of culture as a frame for describing that phenomenon
- To seek the perspectives of people in that setting, most often engaging in open-ended interviewing as one way of obtaining those perspectives
- To serve as a bridge between the people studied and the audience for the report
- To attend to what people do, not just what they say
- To explore the relationships among personal, collective, organizational, and structural dynamics
- To assist in theory development

---

Heyman's research, for example, has consistently been done in the field along the U.S.–Mexico border region in California and Arizona, in such places as Agua Prieta, Sonora, and Douglas, Arizona (1995, p. 261).

Another signature aspect of ethnographic research is the concept of culture. In public administration that concept may assist in examining the internal dynamics of an organization, the relations among the organization and its community, or the community being served or impacted by an administrative agency. Heyman identified three key aspects of the culture concept involved in his ethnographic research into public bureaucracies: (1) a historical perspective, (2) attention to concrete and efficacious mechanisms utilized to socialize employees, and (3) recognition of the ways that work patterns promote group identification (2004, p. 494). His research has also utilized the concept of culture in examining the impact of INS work on the larger culture (1995, 1998), how the INS "is reshaping the class and ethnic landscape of the United States" (1995, p. 277), the ways that INS socialization inculcates the desired worldview among its employees (1995, p. 267), and the degree of cross-national ethnic solidarity expressed by INS and Border Patrol officials of Mexican ancestry (Heyman 2002).

This brings us to the third consideration for when to use a qualitative ethnographic approach. Knowing that ethnography is well suited to exploring the relations among personal, collective, organizational, and structural dynamics, in his research Heyman has gone beyond traditional organizational culture studies approaches to examine the enactment of power relations at personal, organizational, institutional, domestic policy, and international relations levels. One example of his work that brings all of these levels into play is his 2001 article on class and classification. In it he examined the ways that official and unofficial (covert) classifications used by INS officials affect their thinking as well as the thinking of those being classified. This dynamic is multifaceted and affects "their movement, treatment and identities in highly unequal ways" (2001, p. 130). He also looked at how INS classifications contribute to exploitation of undocumented workers, to segmentation of immigrant communities, to implementation of public policy, and to U.S.–Mexico relations.

Interviewing persons inside and outside of the INS, Heyman has attempted to obtain and share the perspectives of people engaged in immigration policy implementation. Inside the INS, his interviews included INS district directors, U.S. Border Patrol chiefs and agents, and INS port-of-entry inspectors. Outside of the INS, Heyman has talked with various players in immigration policy enactment, including lawyers and immigration advocates. Although he has strong opinions about the subject he is studying, it is clear that Heyman has not used his interviewees to speak his mind (cf. Heyman 2002, p. 484, note 6). Instead, he has sought to describe their self-understandings.

Heyman is very aware of his role as a bridge between those he interviews and his audience. For example, in his article on immigration officers of Mexican ancestry (Heyman 2002), he included a note (p. 479, note 2) in which he discussed his use of the term "Hispanic" in the field and in his interviews, but the phrase "of Mexican ancestry" in the article. A key point in his article dealt with the relations between Mexican immigrants and the INS officials of Mexican ancestry. He considered "Hispanic" too generic a term to carry the point he was making, and terms like "Chicano" and "Latino" carry political connotations he wished to avoid. His role as bridge was also evident when he did not take what was said in the interviews at face value (e.g., Heyman 2002, p. 480, note 3).

In the ethnographic tradition, there are many manners of observation that may be characterized by a spectrum ranging from complete participant, to participant-as-observer, to observer-as-participant, to complete observer (Angrosino and Mays de Pérez 2000, p. 675). In the articles referenced, Heyman appears to have been a "complete observer," but his observation did involve lengthy periods in the field. For example, Heyman's 1995 article on the worldviews of INS employees was based on fieldwork that lasted from December 1991 to June 1992. He has also observed INS officials engaged in patrolling the border, administering ports of entry, questioning suspects, raiding workplaces, and appearing in immigration courts (Heyman 2002, p. 484).

Ethnographers rely upon multiple sources of data. The most common in qualitative ethnographic research include observation, semistructured or open-ended interviewing, and reading various documents. Heyman has reported: observing routine operations, e.g., training sessions (physical education, Spanish language, immigration law) and border port operations (including inspections and interrogations); using INS statistics (1995, p. 266, note 11); and examining training materials, e.g., course syllabi and multiple editions of the Spanish textbook utilized by INS (Heyman 1995, p. 268). It is also clear from his articles that he has carefully attended to other related studies.

In addition to interviewing people, and collecting and interpreting multiple sources of data, an ethnographer needs to be attentive to what people do. Understanding what one sees and hears in the field requires thoughtful attention to the differences between official policy, voiced policy, and enacted policy. Public administration researchers are likely to recognize that these aspects of ethnography are similar to our tradition of "implementation studies." Beyond the implications for understanding the nuts and bolts of implementation, Heyman recognizes the value of this kind of attentiveness for larger issues of policy administration and public administration theory: "We ought to bring ethnography, with its Malinowskian virtue of revealing what people do as well as what they say, to bear on the central questions of policy and power" (2004, p. 489).

As is often the case in qualitative research approaches, ethnographic research tends to be rather open-ended, seeking to discover things not known rather than to confirm things already suspected. In that regard, ethnographers often rely upon qualitative approaches to interviewing as a key part of their research; Heyman is no exception to this tendency. He has described his interviews as having a uniform structure that allowed for "elaboration and questioning as the exchange developed" (1995, p. 266). Even more direct evidence that his is an open-ended discovery approach is found in his statement that he has employed "a discovery framework" (1995, p. 263).

Despite the fact that Heyman's project is focused on gathering the perspectives of those involved in implementing immigration policy, he is not reluctant to interpret their perspectives in ways that they may have never considered—and might not agree with. In one article (2002), he described ways that the self-understandings of immigration officers of Mexican ancestry restricted their empathy for Mexican immigrants and facilitated their treatment of those immigrants as "other." Moreover, he suggested that there are ways the self-understandings of the officers are involved with the U.S. public's opposition to immigration. In a more general statement of his use of ethnography to examine bureaucracies, he stated:

> My working assumption is that the results of bureaucratic action are not idiosyncracies or failures but in some way reflections of the combination of various internal and external power relations surrounding the organization, often crystallized into patterns of organizational routine and discretion, as clues to wider political arrangements and governing ideologies. (2004, p. 489)

With respect to immigration officers of Mexican ancestry, he interpreted their failure to empathize with more recent Mexican immigrants as influenced by their struggles to enact their roles as citizens of the United States and members of the INS. Thus, Heyman took their perspectives and treated them with respect, but he did not hesitate to use his intellectual and analytic abilities to assess their implications.

As one might surmise, ethnographic research can also make a valuable contribution to theory development. So, if you are interested in contributing to theory development, ethnography may be an approach you want to utilize. What this means in practice may be more easily understood by specific reference, again, to Heyman's work. In his article on class and classification he stated clearly that he saw his work as contributing to theory development (2001, p. 129). Specifically, he saw this portion of his work contributing to our theoretical understanding of socioeconomic inequality because he delineated ways in which official classifications and informal (covert) class distinctions impacted transfers of and access to valuable resources. His 1995 and 2004 articles about the anthropological study of bureaucracies delineate and demonstrate a contribution that ethnographic research can make to the study of bureaucratic power.

If you have time for field research, an interest in culture or relational dynamics, and/or a desire to assist in developing theories about culture and relational dynamics, learning how to utilize ethnographic approaches will be worth your while.

## Design Issues in Ethnographic Research

Ethnography shares many design issues with other qualitative research approaches, but there are specific ways that those general issues tend to manifest themselves in ethnography. There are also some issues that, although they are not unique to ethnographic research, seem especially important in this approach.

As is the case generally with qualitative research, a research project utilizing an ethnographic approach cannot be fully programmed ahead of time. It is not simply a question of following steps or methodological rules once the instrument is designed (assuming an instrument *is* designed). Typically, design issues will continue to arise and the researcher will continue to rework and modify them throughout the life of the project. Nonetheless, there remains a significant need for preparation and some need for design prior to beginning the project.

Given these preliminary considerations, designing an ethnographic research approach requires attentive consideration of the challenges listed in Box 4.3. A standard step in most any research project is the identification of a problem to be researched. M. Hammersley and P. Atkinson borrow Malinowski's use of the term "foreshadowed problems" to indicate the tentativeness with which an ethnographer may want to endow the problems with which he or she begins a research project (1995, p. 24). Often those foreshadowed problems are suggested by the literature or by theory, but the researcher's manner of using them must remain somewhat flexible in order to gain the most that one can out of a specific study (especially if a researcher is using a grounded theory approach). If you are seeking the perspectives of those in the setting, there may be good reason not to impose a theoretical lens that is alien to that perspective. The task is one of finding a way to take guidance from the literature or from theories and still fairly represent insider perspectives. There is no reason to begin a study, however, if you have no idea what it is you are trying to understand and why it can be seen as a researchable problem.

That researchable problem may simply be a vague notion to explore. For example, a public administration researcher may be curious about what makes an organization successful (or dysfunctional). In the case of a natural experiment, the problem may be to describe how an organization responded to a watershed event. The problem may be current and topical or it may be classic and conceptual (or some combination of those characterizations). Heyman's work is current and topical, but it addresses big concepts. His 1995 and 2002 articles are both aimed at understanding organizational power. In 1995, he focused on the "thought-work" involved in implementing INS classifications in order to "show how the concept of thought-work can be used to reveal organizational power" (p. 261). His 2002 article focused on how notions of citizenship held by INS officers of Mexican ancestry affect their encounters with immigrants and would-be immigrants from Mexico and Central America. He wanted to examine how social, economic, and organizational processes penetrated the lives of the officers and immigrants in ways that affected their access to power and privileges.

In addition to having a clear idea of the problem you want to research, you need to consider what your purpose is in addressing that problem. Depending upon whether you are planning a traditional academic ethnographic research project or an applied one, you will have different general criteria to consider. An academic ethnographic approach will probably need to have a more thoroughly developed theoretical perspective. There will be a tricky balance to reach between originality and grounding in the discipline's research tradition. A major purpose of the research will be to contribute toward development of knowledge in the discipline. An applied research project is likely to be more pragmatic, e.g., informing a specific decision or strategy, empowering a community or group, or promoting a change. Typically it will be less concerned with theory, originality, and development of knowledge in the discipline and more concerned with (1) framing the project in a manner that will be effective for the intended audience, (2) conducting the research in a way that is easy to explain and justify, and (3) supporting the specific social, policy, or administrative actions that motivate the research.

Heyman's work tends toward the traditional academic category, but it carries with it some deliberate pragmatic agendas. He wants to encourage anthropologists to study contemporary problems and to address the power of public bureaucracies. "The techniques of power inhere in the routines of bureaucratic workers and their relationships with the persons they attempt to control" (1995, p. 261). He sees those techniques of power as significant contributing factors in "the global distribution of unequal life chances" (2002, p. 480). In revealing those techniques of power and the ways they contribute to the exploitation of some people for the benefit of others, he seems to hope to make them more difficult to sustain (cf. 2004, p. 497, note 1).

Research questions help organize the data collection and analysis of a specific research project to address the general research problem. They are also a way of breaking the general research problem into more specific problems/questions to be addressed. Each question posed should be related to the research problem so that the answers to the questions help to enlighten us about the problem. One of the research questions Heyman posed in his 2002 article was "how social and economic processes penetrate lives and motivate group identification" (p. 480). He pursued that question by examining the content of INS officials' notions of citizenship and the ways those notions affected their ideas and actions as they encountered potential Mexican immigrants. Those encounters had significant impacts on the life chances of the would-be immigrants. In the 1995 article he pursued the contribution of thought work to the enactment of bureaucratic power by addressing two basic questions:

> How do INS officers deal with defiance and frustration in terms of their worldviews' assumptions about the nature of social action and the characteristics of immigrants as others? What do INS worldviews tell us about abusive and abuse-avoiding behaviors? (p. 267)

Pursuing those questions about defiance, frustration and abuse, he was gaining information about how bureaucratic workers enact power in their routines and relationships. In both articles he was examining the same basic problem of understanding bureaucratic power, but in the two articles he asked different questions about the thinking of INS officials in order to inform us about that power.

But why is ethnography an appropriate research approach for addressing that problem and obtaining answers to those questions? It is not sufficient simply to identify a topic and pursue questions. A researcher must also justify the research approach as an appropriate way to attempt the task. In his 1995 article Heyman provided a direct and clear explanation of why ethnography is an appropriate approach to a better understanding of bureaucratic power:

> Concrete organizations employ techniques of power for specific ends in contexts wider than the bureaucracy itself. The analysis of these techniques is not, however, simply a matter of examining explicit policy and other

**Box 4.3   Ethnographic Design Challenges**

**Identifying your ethnographic research focus**

- identify the general topic(s)/research problems in which you are interested
- establish your research purpose
- articulate your research questions

**Justifying your ethnographic research**

- explain why an ethnographic research approach is appropriate for this project
- explain why you are an appropriate person to do this ethnography
- explain why the specific group that you plan to observe is well-suited for this project
- explain why the specific setting in which you will observe this group is well-suited for this project

**Planning how to do the field study**

- where will the study take place?
- when will the study take place?
- if you are already a member, anticipate the impacts that can have on your research and describe ways of dealing with them
- if you are not a member, anticipate the impact your presence will have
- explain how you will obtain entry
- estimate the amount of time you will spend on site
- decide to what extent you expect to participate while you observe
- plan a respectful and sensitive exit (or transition) strategy

**Planning the analysis and writing**

- determine whether you will generate your analytical frame based on the literature or in a grounded theory fashion
- anticipate what style of writing you might utilize in presenting your study to others

products of power holders, for all too often official goals mystify the real application of organized power. . . .

Ethnography shatters the hard surface of officiality. . . . I can hardly think of a method more inclined to penetrate formalism in the study of power. (pp. 261 and 264–65)

In 2004 Heyman reiterated this justification of "the ethnography of bureaucracy" by arguing that "we have to learn about bureaucracies . . . on the spot, in the midst of engagement" (p. 488). Later in that same article he elaborated on this theme: "The study of bureaucratic thought cannot be isolated as stand-alone 'idea systems' or 'discourses,' but must be observed in performance" (p. 493).

Ethnographic research is not for everyone. There are two levels at which it is reasonable to ask whether you are the appropriate person to do ethnographic research: (1) In general, are you the kind of researcher who is well suited to doing ethnographic research? (2) Are you an appropriate person for a specific ethnographic research project? Ethnographic research often requires a lot of time and always requires someone who can gain access, establish rapport and trust, and deal with people sensitively and with an attitude of appreciation. You must be observant, have a good memory, and be willing to take the time and effort to record your observations. You must enjoy interacting with people and helping them out. You must possess a flexible curiosity and be able to take risks and live with ambiguity. Instead of relying on research techniques to give you confidence in your insights, you need to trust your intuition. (For a more complete exploration of what kind of person should do ethnographic research, see LeCompte and Schensul 1999.)

Even if you are a skilled ethnographer, you may not be an appropriate person for a specific study. Sometimes it is difficult to believe that a person thought he or she could establish the kind of relationship needed for a successful ethnographic study. There have been many instances of first world Caucasian male academics doing ethnographic research on third world tribes, but one might reasonably question the transparency with which the tribal members related to the researchers. When doing ethnographic research in Western bureaucracies or with communities served by them, the characteristics of the researcher may be crucial for the success of the project. For example, an older white male academic is not likely to establish as thorough a rapport and trust with African American women on welfare as a relatively young African American woman. Although this chapter utilizes the work of Josiah Heyman to illustrate most of its points, it is not clear to me how he established his relationship with those he studied, and I have not found a place where he directly explains why he was an appropriate person to engage in ethnographic research on the INS at the U.S.–Mexico border.[2]

Ethnographies most often focus on a group of people in a particular setting. Consequently, the identification of the group to be studied and/ or the setting in which to do the research may have a great impact on the research question. The researcher may have come upon the research question because he or she was in an organization that generated the concern. Conversely, an exciting opportunity to study a question may arise in a specific setting. It could be that the relationship of the researcher to those in the setting provides an unusually promising (or at least very appropriate) opportunity for exploring the research question. The setting also may be important to the research for other reasons—e.g., access, cost, and time considerations. Heyman explained his choice of the U.S.–Mexico border to study the power of bureaucracies by noting, "There is no better place to witness the applications and limits of power than the U.S.–Mexico border" (1995, p. 262). At that border, agents implement decisions affecting who gets into the United States and obtains access to the resources available there.

Because of the importance of fieldwork in ethnographic approaches, your approach to it requires considerable planning and a good design. The first questions to address in this regard are where and when: where will be the fieldwork be set, and when will the research take place? Ethnographic research has a tradition of requiring significant amounts of time in the field, but more rapid procedures are beginning to be developed and accepted (N.S. Scrimshaw and G.R. Gleason 1992). If you are designing a rapid ethnographic research procedure, the setting needs to be one with which you are already familiar and the research problem needs to be tightly focused. If you are a member of the culture you plan to study, there are special challenges that must be faced. Prior familiarity with the setting and the people carries advantages and disadvantages. Entry, access, and rapport may be easier to obtain, but the naïve perspective of the outsider may be difficult to approximate. Participation may be a foregone conclusion, but that may make research-related observation more difficult. For example, if you are doing ethnographic research in the organization for which you work, it will be difficult to find the time in your regular work schedule to develop your field notes. You may not have to develop an exit strategy so much as a transition strategy in which you return to your singular role as a member of the organization no longer engaged in research. If your research is to be presented publicly, the impact of your report on your relations with your organization will need to be dealt with sensitively.

From the moment that you begin to consider a research project you are likely to be setting your analytical frame. The first key decision that you will face is whether to utilize a framework suggested by the literature in the field or one that you develop from your insights into the perspectives of those involved in the study. In his 2001 article on classification, Heyman's framework was more of a grounded theory approach, developing out of the formal and informal categories utilized by the people in the INS. In that analysis, he distinguished the legal categories (citizens, legal immigrants, nonimmigrant visitors, and undocumented migrants), and the informal categories such as moral worth, national origins stereotypes (e.g., "José Mexican"), and apparent social classes. In 2002 he more directly imposed analytical categories based on his expertise. For example, he coded interviews based on whether the interviewees distinguished between ethnicity and citizenship. This is probably not a way of understanding their perspective that his interviewees would have suggested.

In planning the writing of an ethnographic research project, one needs to keep in mind three roles that writing plays: recording, analyzing, and communicating. In an ethnographic approach, writing is not a mechanical process that is confronted only after the data are collected; rather, it is involved in the project from start to finish. The way you record data needs to be consistent with the intended analytical method and the style of communication you expect to utilize. If you intend to use a grounded theory approach, you need to take extensive verbatim notes. If you expect to present quotations from open-ended interviews, you will probably need to record and transcribe those interviews. Most people cannot keep up with the conversation and take verbatim quotes at the same time. If you intend to present your findings through thick description, you will need to train yourself to take effective field notes of your observations.

Perhaps it is because he is an academic, but Heyman tends to write a lot about where his work fits in the literature and why his approach is important to the field. He spent a lot of time and energy interviewing INS managers and officers (1995, p. 265, note 11), so his writing includes much attention to those interviews and sometimes extensive direct quotations from them (e.g., 1995, 1998, 2002). Accounts of his observations, though, are relatively rare—and often include more attention to what he heard than what he saw, smelled, or tasted (e.g., 2001, pp. 132–33). Given his research purpose, this seems appropriate. So, I do not mean to criticize his writing, but in order to see examples of the use of thick description in ethnography, one must look elsewhere.[3]

Having identified your research focus, justified the appropriateness of your research approach, made plans for your field study, and anticipated the style of writing you want to use, you are ready to work on the logistical issues you will face.

**Logistical Issues**

Ethnographic research approaches also entail some important logistical issues that need to be considered very early in the project. Generally, they involve making sure that you can gain access to the necessary people and data (see Box 4.4). (Since ethnographies are sometimes considered a kind of case study, there is considerable overlap between this list of things to consider and the one presented in Chapter 5 [Box 5.4].)

In ethnography, it may be difficult to separate your need for data from your need for relationships with people who can assist you with your research project. In order to understand a group's culture you need to observe what people do and listen to what they say—both as they are acting and when they ascribe meaning to their actions.

First, let's address the issue of access to people. Without access to people, ethnographic research is not possible. The key to access is relationships. In general the kind of relationship that is often recommended for an ethnographic researcher is described as an integrated outsider maintaining "ethnographic marginality" (R.M. Emerson, R.I Fretz, and L.L. Shaw 1995, p. 35.) "Fieldwork asks the researcher, as far as possible, to share firsthand the environment, problems, background, language, rituals, and social relations of a more-or-less bounded and specified group of people" (Van Maanen 1988, p. 3). An ethnographic researcher typically needs an attitude of appreciation toward the experiences of those being studied, but that does not mean that she/he has to accept their viewpoints—only that he/she has empathy for them.

It would not be sufficient for an ethnographer to gain access to people in the group. In order to obtain the kind of information and insight needed, an ethnographer needs to establish rapport and trusting relationships.

**Box 4.4   Logistical Challenges in Qualitative Ethnographic Research**

**Who are the people from whom you need assistance/ information?**

- community or organization members?
- others who regularly work with or in relation to the community or organization?
- other experts (consultants, government officials)?

**Do you have a way of gaining access to them?**

- already established relationships?
- friends, acquaintances, colleagues, contacts who can help to access them?
- reason to believe they will be willing to assist?

**What are the data sources you need to access/create?**

- interviews?
- field observations?
- organizational documents?
- other studies or reports?

Often, entry to a group is facilitated by a specific member, but who that member is can open some doors and close others. Even if the person who helps you gain entry is well regarded by all other members, you still must establish your own relationships with them. A nonjudgmental attitude seems to be a minimum requirement for this to take place.

It is not clear how Heyman gained access to and established rapport with people in the field setting, but he has provided several insights into his relationships with INS officers. Admitting that he did not share their immigration-restrictionist position, he said he was "drawn to the present subject not by a desire to judge and condemn but by a great interest in and sympathy with officers' use of governmental jobs and state machinery to render their lives decent and secure" (2002, p. 484, note 6). He also recognized that his interviewees sometimes colored their responses in order to present themselves as more empathetic toward immigrants than their total pattern of thinking would indicate (2002, p. 480, note 3). In contrast to that, he went out of his way to describe the INS stereotypes of Mexicans as "generally favorable" (1998, p. 176, note 7), to note the infrequency of INS human rights abuses (1995, p. 267, note 15), and to absolve INS managers of responsibility for what he described as appalling work conditions (1995, p. 271, note 24).

Much of the data you need will be generated in connection with your relationships and interactions with the people of the community or organization. Your data is likely to include both organized interviews and in-the-field conversations with members. As was mentioned earlier, one of the central features of ethnographic research is observation in the field. Recording those observations is crucial to the development of an ethnographic research approach. Writing field notes is the most common way of recording ethnographic observational data. In some circumstances it is also possible to make audio or video recordings, but even if that is the case the researcher will eventually have to transform those recordings into text. Audio recordings may be transcribed, but video recordings require notes that address the visual data as well as the words recorded.

Clearly the data gathered from the field is at the heart of an ethnographic research approach, but an ethnographer may need to triangulate or put that data into context by utilizing other sources of information. Those sources may include organizational documents, newspaper articles (or other news media accounts), and/or other studies or reports. Heyman has used organizational documents from the INS, media accounts from sources such as the *Los Angeles Times, New York Times,* and *Harper's,* and other studies on subjects such as racism, immigration, citizenship, border communities, and street-level bureaucracy.

Having addressed the logistical challenges related to people, in-the-field observation, and document collection, you are ready to enter the field to create and collect data.

**Collecting and Creating Data**

The researcher herself or himself is designedly (and inevitably) the most important research instrument involved in ethnographic research. The researcher's whole being is involved in and affects the gathering of data. Ethnographic research recognizes that its validity does not rely upon distancing the researcher from the collection of data through the use of mechanical collection techniques. An ethnographer's personality and other characteristics affect what he or she is able to observe and what people will say, do, or otherwise reveal in the course of the research study. Moreover, ethnographic research approaches rely on the researcher's observational skills in attending to things in the field and good judgment in deciding what data to collect.

Observation is a key feature of ethnographic research. It entails attending to the physical setting, what people say and do, and the nature of their relationships. It requires that you watch, listen (even eavesdrop), and question. But no one can see, hear, taste, smell, or feel everything around them. That means you will be, in effect, editing the experience right from the beginning. You want your reduced version of the experience to capture the important and meaningful aspects of what you observe.

In order to turn your observations into data, you need to have some idea what to attend to and what to take note of. What you have observed does not become data until you make a note about it. Initially, the plethora of potential data may be overwhelming, so it may be helpful to put together a format that helps organize your collection of it. Thus begins the editing. It may be somewhat mechanical at first, but gradually an ethnographic researcher begins to gain confidence and uses those mechanical techniques to help focus attention but does not allow them to prevent taking note of important aspects of the observations. E. Chiseri-Strater and B.S. Sunstein (2001) have provided a list of the kinds of things that might well be included in all field notes. The list could be used to set up a format for your field notes. It includes date, time, place, specific observations (numbers, details), impressions, specific words or phrases, conversation summaries, and questions for future consideration.

Whether you utilize such a mechanical manner of note taking or not, you will need to create some way of taking field notes. It may be tempting to think of field notes as jotting words onto a pad small enough to be carried around, but ethnographic field notes are not so simple a matter. There are many kinds of field notes: mental notes, quick scratch notes (taken in the midst of observing), longer notes (written in breaks from the action), and more composed notes (often written in the evening, perhaps as journals or diaries). In this list the latter kinds build upon the earlier ones. For example, one might take a mental note to remember something observed until there is an opportunity to record it as a scratch note, which will later be elaborated into a longer note that will form the grist for composing more thoughtful notes when there is time to reflect upon the observations while they are relatively fresh. The purpose of the words jotted in the scratch notes is to help remember scenes when you compose more elaborate notes later. As you move from scratch notes to more composed notes, you are also moving from data generation to analysis. This simple structure of progressive note taking provides a way to preserve the details of observations so that they are not forgotten or overlooked as you build your analysis.

When writing field notes you need to record your immediate observations and impressions. Although it may sometimes be difficult to know what they are when you see them, it is important to focus on key events. You may simply have to trust your sense of what is key, while keeping in mind that if your goal is empathetic understanding you need to attend to what it appears that others see as key. You need to move beyond personal reactions and note what members of the group see as significant. What do they attend to, react to, and talk about? Still, you should not deny personal reactions—and you should take note of them. In writing notes, you should avoid generalizations and provide specifics. You should also avoid evaluative, opinionated words because when they are read later they tend to evoke only vague memories. Instead, write down sensory details (e.g., gestures, postures, eye movements) and actual words and phrases uttered. Avoid ascribing motives, but note emotions by describing how they are expressed. Notes should help you remember, so write down things that you might otherwise forget. (For a much more thorough source of advice on writing field notes, see Emerson, Fretz, and Shaw 1995.)

Approaches to interviewing in ethnographic research are so similar to those discussed in the chapter on qualitative interviewing that I will not repeat them here. There is, however, one significant difference, and it involves the use of informal conversations as sources of data. In ethnographic research, informal conversations are an important part of the data that is collected in your field notes. In such conversations, people may be more open and/or comfortable. They might, therefore, provide insights and meanings that you could not obtain in an interview setting. You probably will not want to interrupt the flow of informal conversations by pulling out a pad or piece of paper to write a note, so those notes will depend somewhat on your ability to remember what was said and on your discipline in writing them down as soon as you find an appropriate opportunity.

Another important source of information for ethnographic research in the field of public administration is likely to be documents, organizational files, or other written records. Written records are key artifacts in modern organizational life—indeed, in any literate social activity—but they are at the heart of bureaucratic organizational activity and are often seen as the official version of events as the documentation of "reality."

Reports, memos, emails, and other official documents can indicate quite a bit about the operations of a modern organization. In order to do a proper ethnographic account of the culture of such an organization, a researcher must examine and interpret them. Moreover, the researcher must attempt to gain some insight into how those in the organization produce, read, interpret, and use those documents. Hammersley and Atkinson have suggested some of the questions a researcher should ask about documents:

> How are documents written? How are they read? Who writes them? Who reads them? For what purposes? On what occasions? With what outcomes? What is recorded? What is omitted? What does the writer seem to take for granted about the reader(s)? What do readers need to know in order to make sense of them? (1995, p. 173).

In addition to official documents, an ethnographic researcher should be on the lookout for such informal written records as personal diaries, journals, or letters. Reports from outsiders (e.g., media reports or other studies) may also be useful. These documents may not be central to the functioning of a bureaucracy, but they can provide important perspectives on them.

When you find documentary data, you may face some challenges in getting them recorded in a manner useful for your research. Sometimes it is easy to photocopy or scan them, but other times getting them recorded requires taking notes or reading them into a recorder and transcribing later. It may even be necessary to simply summarize them in your own words.

Heyman's use of documentary evidence was vital to his 2001 article on class and classification. His treatment of classifications addressed formal and informal categories and "the interplay between them" (2001, p. 129). The formal classifications he identified included: citizens, legal immigrants, nonimmigrant visitors, and undocumented migrants. Among the informal classifications he recognized were: moral worth, national origins stereotypes, and apparent social class. He looked not only at the classifications, but how they were interpreted, applied, enacted, believed, and/or ignored. He recognized that INS classifications meant different things to INS officials, immigrants, and the general U.S. citizenry. Because the formal documentary record often did not resolve the situation, INS officials relied on intense verbal interrogations to interpret the

---

**Box 4.5   Common Sources of Ethnographic Data**

- observation
- interviews
- informal conversations
- personal diaries, records, letters, or other documents
- organizational files and documents
- media reports
- other studies related to the community or organization

---

evidence they had on a potential immigrant into "plausible stories" (p. 132). In general, Heyman concluded that "the suspicious tone of domestic immigration politics, the public notion that fraud and illegality lurks among migrants, bypasses the right-and-powers aspect of formal law to pervade the actual practice of INS covert classification" (p. 136).

Ethnographic data collection and generation depends in part upon qualitative interviewing. To that it adds observing and interacting in the field, and reading various kinds of written documents (see Box 4.5). Because ethnographic research is focused on the enactment of culture, it depends most centrally upon observation and interaction. Having observed, interacted, conversed, interviewed, and read, the next task is to analyze the data that those activities created.

**Analyzing It**

There are many ways to do analysis (see Box 4.6). All of them involve closely examining the data and "thinking up" from the specific data toward more general ideas in order to make meaning of them. The chapter on qualitative interviewing addressed ways of analyzing interviews, and the chapter on narrative inquiry included a section on analysis of stories obtained through interviewing. The chapter on case studies will delineate specific activities involved with examining the data, thinking up, and making meaning (see Chapter 5, Box 5.6), so this chapter will not repeat that material. Here I will address aspects of analyzing ethnographic data, focusing on data deriving from in-the-field observation and interaction.

---

**Box 4.6    What Ethnographic Analysis Involves**

- translating your observations and interactions into notes
- if you include interviews, making transcriptions of them
- revisiting your notes and interview transcriptions frequently
- deciding how much to emphasize description, explanation, and argumentation in organizing your coded materials
- deciding whether your concepts will be formed through grounded theory or abstract theory imported from the literature
- sorting and grouping your codes
- noting surprises, puzzles, and metaphors
- using concepts and themes to code your notes and transcriptions
- deciding whether to utilize multiple theoretical frames
- continuing to reconsider your codes and create new ones
- organizing your coded materials for use in writing your manuscript

---

When you design a study, you are beginning your analysis. Having a notion that you can explore or examine a general problem by looking at a specific setting means that you expect the specifics you observe to have meaning in relation to a more general idea. Analysis is the task of identifying the meaning of the specifics you observe for the general research problem you decided to study.

As was mentioned earlier, as soon as you begin to translate your observations into notes, you have begun analyzing—but good analysis is not a rigid, mechanical process. It is reflective and recursive. You will need to revisit your notes and transcriptions many times. Some of your beginnings are not going to be significant parts of your final analysis, and some of them are going to be central. You may not know which will be which until you are pretty deep into the analysis. That is not a problem. It is normal and an inherent function of reflective thinking because it requires you to go back and reconsider and reframe what you have previously been thinking about. As Fetterman has pointed out: "First and foremost, analysis is a test of the ethnographer's ability to think" (1998, p. 93).

Analysis can be thought of as descriptive, explanative, or argumentative. Some analysis is more focused on making a general point, and some of it is more focused on weaving specifics together in a way that feels "true to the experience." The farther you allow yourself to move away from the specifics, the more you are engaged in explanation and/ or argumentation. The closer you remain to the specifics, the more you may be said to be engaged in description. All analytic methods, however, require interpretation—making meaning of the specifics. Sometimes the meaning is implied through the flow of a story. Sometimes it is developed through comparison and contrast to a model or ideal. Other times it is categorized into typologies, or used to construct or explain a model.

If the concepts you use derive from the participants in the local setting, you are doing what some call "grounded theory" (A. Strauss and J. Corbin 1990). As mentioned earlier, Heyman's 2001 article on class and classification is an example of the use of grounded theory. If the concepts you use derive from the literature or from your own ideas or arguments that you impose on your data, you are using abstract theory. Heyman's 2002 article on immigration officers of Mexican ancestry is an example of using theory from the literature. In it he used his ethnographic research to contribute to citizenship theory. From the content of that article it appears that he emphasized argumentation in organizing his codes: "My central argument is that internal struggles to achieve substantive citizenship result in institutionally delivered rights and redistributions that shape external politics of inclusion and exclusion of new immigrants from such rights and redistributions" (2002, p. 483). Heyman's 1995 article is another example of using concepts and categories from the literature:

> In categorizing worldviews, I use Kearney's (1984) seven universals: self, other(s), relationship and causality . . . , time, space . . . , and classification. Rather than force artificial consistency on individual conversations, I also utilize Strauss's (1990) classification of mutually contradictory propositions in interviews. (1995, p. 266)

He also used grounded theory categories. His delineation of three tacit policies used by the INS (voluntary departure, differentiation by nationality, and narcotics law enforcement) derived from his fieldwork. In that article, he appears to have emphasized explanation in organizing his material. His work does not provide a good example of description as an emphasis in organizing ethnographic material.

Whether you use a grounded or abstract theory framework (or mix the two) everyone has to use theory and concepts to make sense of their data. Making sense of the data begins with immersing oneself in it, sorting and grouping items, and finding patterns by comparing and contrasting, by recognizing similarities, and/or by noting surprises, puzzles, or metaphors. Sorting and grouping, as well as finding patterns, are done through coding and depend upon larger concepts that help identify similarities and differences. Noting surprises, puzzles, and metaphors also depends upon larger concepts, but sometimes the concept is not a conscious aspect of your thinking until the surprise, puzzle, or metaphor brings it into your awareness. Heyman's 2000 article on immigration officers' moral evaluations of immigrants offers an example of the role of puzzles in giving rise to theoretical frames. In it he identifies his puzzlement regarding INS officers' seemingly contradictory positions on the actions of illegal immigrants as a prime factor in generating his analysis:

> I long puzzled over an unexpected juxtaposition in the rhetoric of INS officers. An experienced officer of second-generation Mexican ancestry said, "If I was in Mexico and starving, the Border Patrol would have hell catching me." This came directly after he referred to recent immigrants as trash (using a Spanish word) and said, "I wonder when the American public is going to realize that it has to put an end to this [extensive immigration] sometime." (2000, p. 640)

A common task in ethnography is coding specific lines in field notes or interview transcripts to identify which concepts they relate to or illustrate. Coding involves using "a word or short phrase that captures and signals what is going on in a piece of data in a way that links it to some more general analytic issue" (Emerson, Fretz, and Shaw 1995, p. 146). In the just mentioned example from Heyman, he must have had the quotes coded under some term related to "moral evaluation." When the concepts are more tentative and used to suggest directions for thought and exploration or to give a temporary point of reference, they may be considered "sensitizing concepts" (H. Blumer 1954). When they are more fixed and not so tentative, they may be considered "definitive concepts." The two terms are not sides on a dichotomy as much as ends of a spectrum representing the degree of confidence one has in the value of the concepts for the analysis being done. One way of using definitive concepts or well-defined theories that still provides for some flexibility is to utilize multiple theoretical frames and explore what each brings into more clear focus. As the analysis proceeds, you will most likely develop more confidence in the concepts that you continue to use.

The work of analysis and reflection will continue as you begin to write a manuscript designed to share your research with some audience. The codes, categories, and theories you began with may or may not be well suited to the perspective you want to present in your manuscript. If they are, you will organize them for use in the manuscript. If they are not, you will need to revisit your notes, recode, and reorganize your coded materials for use in your manuscript.

## Writing It

As was mentioned earlier, when you begin to translate your observations into notes, you have begun writing your ethnographic study. Writing is not just the work you do on the manuscript. The manuscript is dependent upon the field notes and other material you have collected. It is also dependent upon the analysis you do. None of these activities is clearly separate from the others. They are all mutually interdependent. Consequently, this section will begin with brief treatments of the writing that is done in data collection and analysis, but most of it will focus on the task of composing the ethnographic manuscript.

Writing is one of the activities that distinguishes the participant observer from the other members of the group or community being studied in an ethnographic project. The activity of writing, however, is a visible manifestation of the different role the researcher has in the group as compared to the other members. It represents the analytical perspective of the researcher. Writing field notes tends to emphasize description (rather than explanation or argumentation), but no one can avoid having an interpretive perspective when taking those notes. Writing cannot capture and fully represent an event. As C. Geertz has said, an ethnographer turns "a passing event, which exists only in its own moment of occurrence, into an account, which exists in its inscription and can be reconsulted" (1973, p. 19). Reduction is an inevitable aspect of this writing, but recording an event in field notes counteracts the reduction to some degree; recording adds to the details in your accounts of the passing events so that they can more accurately be remembered and reconsidered.

Your writing becomes further detached from the events as you consciously analyze your observations. Some of this is likely to happen when you are taking time away from the field to write up your recent observations from your notes, memories, and impressions. Whether your extended notes take the form of a single paragraph, a sketch, an episode, or a story, they organize the relatively chaotic experience into a description that is more meaningful for you (and later for your readers, if you decide to include it in the final manuscript). Ethnographic researchers often write memos to themselves as a further step in analyzing the data. Those memos are conscious attempts to analyze the data in ways that suggest their connection to the larger concepts being studied.

To the degree that your purpose involves the presentation of insider perspectives, your analytic writing will be aimed at describing and explaining their views. To the degree that your purpose involves presenting a group or community from an outsider's perspective, your analytic writing will be aimed at supporting your explanation or argument.

When it comes time to begin composing your ethnographic manuscript, you are moving from writing for yourself to writing for an audience. The task is basically one of presenting the group or community you have studied in a way that makes sense to readers who have no direct acquaintance with it. In order to do that, you will need to move back and forth between the specifics in your data and the concepts and theories you are using to organize your presentation. Exactly how you do that will depend upon whether you have a descriptive, explanative, or argumentative purpose and whether you adopt a thematic essay or story-based writing mode.

In some fields, authors are beginning to be creative in the ways they present their ethnographic research. Public administration is not yet one of those fields. Most public administration related ethnographic manuscripts begin with an introduction that tells the reader what to expect and introduces the writer's main concerns. Although Heyman usually does not label the first portion of his articles with the term "introduction," that is what they are. His 2001 article on class and classification begins by discussing the connection between U.S. immigration policy implementation and class. Then it explains the relation between class and classification and offers a brief explanation of how the article will elucidate that relationship.

The introduction is commonly followed by a section that links this work to other research (the literature review). The "Approaching Classification" section in Heyman's 2001 article addresses how anthropology has defined and dealt with the term *classification,* but

---

**Box 4.7   Two Ethnographic Manuscript Models**

**Thematic Essay**

Introduction

Literature Review

Methods, Setting, and Researcher Role

Findings Presented in Explanatory or Argumentative
  Fashion

Conclusion

**Story-based Essay**

Introduction

Literature Review

Methods, Setting, and Researcher Role

Findings Presented Through Stories

Conclusion

---

it also continues explicating how Heyman plans to address class and classification in the article.

Next comes some description of the group, the setting, the researcher's role in the group, and the research methods utilized. Heyman tends not to include a section of this sort. Instead, when he addresses these topics, they are likely to appear woven into his articles, or even relegated to footnotes or endnotes. His 2002 article on immigration officers of Mexican ancestry contains notes where he has provided information about his methods and the setting (e.g., notes 2, 3, and 8). Breaking from the model suggested for ethnographic studies, he does not directly address his role in the communities and organizations he has studied (but it appears that he was a nonparticipant observer).

It is the heart of the manuscript that most clearly differs depending on whether you are writing a thematic essay or a story-based essay (see Box 4.7). Both the thematic essay and the story-based essay are ways of analyzing the data. The thematic essay is often deliberately explanatory or argumentative and is guided more by the themes and concepts. Its structure often is guided by logical patterns that are used to attribute causation or to identify patterns. The story-based essay appears more descriptive; however, because the structure of a story implies causal linkages, it is also explanatory. The structure of the story-based manuscript is guided by literary conventions about how a story is told. In most professional or academic writing, the story-based or essay mode findings are usually followed by a conclusion that reflects the introduction and briefly reconnects ideas presented in the thematic essay or story mode.

Depending upon whether the themes derive from the literature or from grounded theory, a thematic essay may be driven more by the ideas and interests of the researcher than the perspectives of those being studied. If you choose the thematic essay structure, it should be guided by the themes or concepts that you want to address. The themes will need to be illustrated and/or supported by material from your notes. For example, you may use excerpts from your field notes to illustrate a point. You may also choose to summarize material from your notes. Verbatim quotes and thick descriptions of events and settings are typical features of ethnographic writing. The more different the actual text in your manuscript is from your notes, the more likely it is that you are imposing your own views, rather than presenting the perspectives of the members of the group you have studied.

A story-based essay is better at presenting insider perspectives. If you choose the story mode, the structure will more likely be guided by chronology and the content will be closely tied to your field notes. Because it is more closely tied to the field notes, it tends to present in more detail what people in the group said or did. Those details need to be presented in a literary fashion, including such elements as characterization and dramatic tension to develop a compelling story line. The details should include such things as typical situations, dramatic moments, evocative portrayals, and telling dialogues. Other than chronology and literary conventions, the general organizational driver will be the topic you are addressing or point you want to make. That general organizational driver helps you to select which portions of your field notes are included and which are not. As Emerson, Fretz, and Shaw have said, in writing a story you "must conceptualize the relevance of local happenings so that they relate to analytical issues" (1995, p. 174) while attempting not to let the analytics overwhelm sensitive presentation of insider perspectives. It is necessary to package the stories with interpretive commentary, but that interpretation should be empathetic to members' perspectives, not a wiser-than-thou outsider perspective.

Of course you could also choose some other way of writing up your ethnographic research. This text is not the place to explore all of the possibilities. It may be sufficient here to point out that you could use vignettes and extended quotations from conversations or interviews to support an explanatory or argumentative essay, thus mixing the two manuscript forms addressed above as Heyman has. For example, in the 2001 article, in order to describe how immigration officers enact covert classifications, he tells a story about an interrogation that he observed (pp. 132–33). In the 1995 and 2002 articles he utilizes many direct quotations to support his analysis of the thoughts of immigration officers of Mexican ancestry as they implement U.S. policy.

Finally, in the same way that the organization and presentation of the manuscript is aimed at developing an effective relationship with your reader, the details utilized in it should be presented in a manner that is respectful of the members of the group being written about. Your foremost concern should be to do no harm to them. If their identities need to be hidden, because an ethnographic study involves people, places, and events in ways that qualitative interviewing does not, it may not be sufficient to change their names. You may need to change the name of the location, organization, and other details in order to keep the participants from being recognizable. In order to be sure that they are comfortable with the way you have presented them, it is good practice to have them review the manuscript prior to sharing it with any other audience. If they are not comfortable with your manuscript, more editing and additional opportunities for them to review the manuscript will be necessary. You have the final say as to what you write, but if you do not treat the members with respect, you have failed in a key aspect of ethnographic research.

## Conclusion

Ethnographic research is an excellent way for public administrators to find out how their programs impact others. It can make significant contributions to implementation research in general and program evaluation in particular.

Like qualitative interviewing and narrative inquiry, ethnographic research provides a view into the world of others. Unlike the first two approaches, however, ethnography involves a researcher in direct experience of that world. It also focuses more on culture as a frame for understanding and is particularly well suited for examining relational dynamics.

Whether your research purpose is academic or pragmatic, it will help if you are clear about your research purpose and specific about the questions to be pursued. Where you do the research and whom you study should be decided in relation to your purpose and your questions.

As a research approach that examines relational dynamics, ethnography involves the researcher in those dynamics. Access, trust, and empathy are crucial for the connection needed to better understand the people and the culture you are studying. Even if you are an outsider, the relations do not end when the study is done or published.

Ethnographic research also involves a lot of writing. From design notes to field notes to publishable manuscript, writing that is clear, specific, and effective is crucial to the success of the project. Interpretation and analysis are inevitably part of the writing. When you take notes on your observation and experiences you are translating them into words that you hope will capture their flavor and meaning.

Clearly, public administration can benefit from more ethnographic research. In order to maximize that benefit, the research needs to be empathetic, sensitive, and appreciative of those being studied. It also needs to be intelligently analyzed and well written.

### Notes

1. He has also published research on the cultures of border communities, but this chapter will not reference that portion of his work.
2. When I contacted Heyman to share an early draft of this chapter with him, he expressed an interest in seeing it, but he never responded with any comments on the chapter in general or on this issue in particular.
3. Chapter 2, "A Day in the Life," of Harry Wolcott's *The Man in the Principal's Office* (1973) is a fine example of thick description. Another example is found in Aldo Leopold's "July" portion of *A Sand County Almanac* (1966). There are many examples of thick description in Leopold's book, but a good brief one that relates to the actions of government agents can be found in his account of what has happened to cutleaf *Silphium*, a plant in the sunflower family that once thrived with the American bison (pp. 48–50).

### Exercises

1. Imagine a research project that you think might be pursued through ethnographic research. Using Box 4.2, explain how your imagined project fits the criteria for when to use an ethnographic approach.
2. Imagine an ethnographic research project that would benefit by being done by **you**. What attitudes, skills, abilities, and other qualities make **you** an appropriate person to undertake this project?

3. Think of an ethnographic research project and explain why the people and the setting are appropriate for it.

4. Using the "planning how to do the field study" section of Box 4.3, address each of the items in relation to the project you discussed in Exercise #3.

5. With reference to that same project, address all the items in Box 4.4.

6. Go to a bus station, train station, airport, shopping mall, or other public setting to observe people. As you watch, listen, etc., scribble notes about what you observe. After about 15 minutes, go to a quieter location and take more extensive notes, sometimes elaborating on the scribbled notes, sometimes adding things you remember that you did not have time to put in a scribbled note. Repeat this exercise several times.

7. Do Exercise #6 with one or more friends or colleagues. Do not communicate with each other about your notes until you each have independently elaborated on them in a quieter setting. Discuss the differences in what you put into your notes. How much of the difference was a function of what you observed? How much a function of what you remembered to put in your notes?

8. Use the field notes generated in Exercise #6 and code them.
   a. You may want to code the field notes using categories that come from your interest or from the literature.
   b. Alternatively, you may attempt to allow the categories you use in the coding to come from the notes (in a grounded theory approach).

## Recommended Readings

Brower, Ralph S., and Mitchel Y. Abolafia. 1997. Bureaucratic politics: The view from below. *Journal of Public Administration Research and Theory,* 7(2): 305–31.

Emerson, R.M., R.I. Fretz, and L.L. Shaw. 1995. *Writing Ethnographic Fieldnotes.* Chicago: University of Chicago Press.

Kaufman, H. 1960/2006. *The Forest Ranger: A Study in Administrative Behavior.* Special reprint ed. Washington, DC: RFF Press.

LeCompte, M.D., and J.J. Schensul. 1999. *Designing and Conducting Ethnographic Research.* Walnut Creek, CA: AltaMira Press.

Leopold, A. 1966. *A Sand County Almanac: With Essays on Conservation from Round River.* New York: Ballantine Books.

Lipskey, M. 1980. *Street Level Bureaucracy: Dilemmas of the Individual in Public Services.* New York: Sage Publications.

Skolnick, J. 1966. *Justice Without Trial: Law Enforcement in Democratic Society.* New York: Wiley.
Wolcott, H.F. 1973. *The Man in the Principal's Office: An Ethnography.* New York: Holt, Rinehart and Winston.

## Recommended Web Site

The Center for Ethnography at the University of California, Irvine. http://www. socsci.uci.edu/~ethnog/.

## References

Angrosino, M., and K.A. Mays de Pérez. 2000. Rethinking observation: From method to context. In *Handbook of Qualitative Research,* ed. N.K. Denzin and Y.S. Lincoln, 673–702. Thousand Oaks, CA: Sage Publications.
Berg, B.L. 2004. *Qualitative Research Mthods for the Social Sciences,* 5th ed. Boston: Pearson Education.
Blumer, H. 1954. What is wrong with social theory? *American Sociological Review,* 19: 3–10.
Chiseri-Strater, E., and B.S. Sustein. 2001. *Fieldworking: Reading and Writing Research.* 2d ed. New York: St. Martin's Press.
Creswell, J.W. 1998. *Qualitative Inquiry and Research Design: Choosing Among Five Traditions.* Thousand Oaks, CA: Sage Publications.
Emerson, R.M., R.I. Fretz, and L.L. Shaw. 1995. *Writing Ethnographic Fieldnotes.* Chicago: University of Chicago Press.
Fetterman, D.M. 1998. *Ethnography: Step by Step.* 2d ed. Thousand Oaks, CA: Sage Publications.
Flick, U. 1999. Qualitative methods in the study of culture and development: An introduction. *Social Science Information,* 38(4): 631–58.
Geertz, C. 1973. *The Interpretation of Cultures.* New York: Basic Books.
Hammersley, M., and P. Atkinson. 1995. *Ethnography: Principles in Practice.* 2d ed. New York: Routledge.
Heyman, J. McC. 1998. State effects on labor exploitation: The INS and undocu-mented immigrants at the Mexico–United States border. *Critique of Anthropol-ogy,* 18(2): 157–80.
———. 2000. Respect for outsiders? Respect for the law? The moral evaluation of high-scale issues by U.S. immigration officers. *Journal of the Royal Anthropo-logical Institute,* N.S., 6: 635–52.
———. 2004. The anthropology of power-wielding bureaucracies. *Human Orga-nization,* 63(4): 487–500.
Kaufman, H. 1960/2006. *The Forest Ranger: A Study in Administrative Behavior.* Special reprint ed. Washington, DC: RFF Press.
Kearney, Michael. 1984. *World view.* Novato, CA: Chandler and Sharp.
LeCompte, M.D. and J.J. Schensul. 1999. *Designing and Conducting Ethnographic Research.* Walnut Creek, CA: AltaMira Press.
Leopold, A. 1966. *A Sand County Almanac: With Essays on Conservation from Round River.* New York: Ballantine Books.

Lipskey, M. 1980. *Street Level Bureaucracy: Dilemmas of the Individual in Public Services.* New York: Sage Publications.

Scrimshaw, N.S., and G.R. Gleason, eds. 1992. *RAP: Rapid Assessment Procedures: Qualitative Methodologies for Planning and Evaluation of Health-Related Programmes.* Boston: INFDC.

Spradley, J.P. 1979. *The Ethnographic Interview.* New York: Holt, Rinehart and Winston.

Strauss, A., and J. Corbin. 1990. *Basics of Qualitative Research: Grounded Theory Procedures and Techniques.* Newbury Park, CA: Sage Publications.

Strauss, Claudia. 1990. Who gets ahead? Cognitive responses to heteroglossia in American political culture. *American Ethnologist,* 17: 312–28.

U.S. General Accounting Office. 2003. *Federal Programs: Ethnographic Studies Can Inform Agencies' Actions.* Washington, DC: U.S. General Accounting Office. GAO-03–455.

Van Maanen, J. 1988. *Tales of the Field: On Writing Ethnography.* Chicago: University of Chicago Press.

# —5—

# Qualitative Case Study Approaches

In public administration, the case study approach is one of the most often used research methods.[1] Professional journals frequently publish case studies. Most of them are qualitative case studies, but case studies may rely upon or emphasize either qualitative or quantitative data. There are also many book-length case studies that are considered classics in public administration literature. Again, they are typically qualitative research but may also include quantitative data.

In this chapter, I first discuss several definitions of the case study approach. The label is widely applied and (I think) often misused, but there are some common features one might reasonably expect to find in a case study. Next, I discuss a variety of types of case studies. Then I address some of the challenges that need to be confronted in doing a case study, beginning with design issues, then logistical issues, collecting and creating data, analyzing that data, and writing the case study composition.

As was the case in Chapters 2, 3, and 4, throughout this chapter I utilize exemplars of the qualitative case study approach published in journals that address issues related to public administration (see Box 5.1). The articles referred to here come from one of the mainstream public administration journals, *Public Administration Review.* **Thompson**'s is an award-winning article on the National Performance Review's reinvention lab program.[2] **Johnston and Romzek** offer a study of Medicaid reform in Kansas. These two articles are among the best journal article case studies I have found and provide good illustrations of many (but not all) of the concepts, issues, and challenges discussed in this chapter.

---

**Box 5.1 Exemplar Articles**

Johnston, J.M., and B.S. Romzek. 1999. Contracting and
accountability in state Medicaid reform: Rhetoric,
theories, and reality. *Public Administration Review,*
59(5): 383–99.

Thompson, J.R. 1999. Devising administrative reform that
works: The example of the reinvention lab program.
*Public Administration Review,* 59(4): 283–92.

---

## Defining the Case Study Approach

Even a cursory review of the case studies published in public administration journals will quickly indicate that many different kinds of research are given the label "case study." Sometimes that label is justified; sometimes it is not. Just because someone refers to an article or chapter as a case study does not mean that it fits any reasonable definition of that approach to research. Too often it appears that the label is used simply because it allows great flexibility in the approach utilized and it provides an answer to the question, What kind of research did you do?

In this chapter, I present several examples of definitions of "case study" that may help to clarify what the approach is. None of them should be considered a final or official definition, but each of them will help to explain what people do when they make conscientious attempts to do qualitative case study research.

H. Stein defined a case study as:

> a narrative of the events that constitute or lead to a decision or group of related decisions by a public administrator or group of public administrators. Some account is given of the numerous personal, legal, institutional, political, economic and other factors that surround the process of decision but there is no attempt to assert absolute causal relationships. (1952, p. xxvii)

An important aspect of this definition is its attention to context—"the numerous . . . factors that surround." The reinvention lab and Kansas Medicaid articles illustrate this attention to context. In **Johnston and Romzek**, the section on "Contracting for social services: The case of Medicaid services for the elderly in Kansas" (pp. 384–85) places their case study in the context of Kansas's "wide ranging privatization efforts" for a variety of social services. This article also utilizes its "Notes" section to elaborate on various contextual elements (cf. p. 386, notes 3 and 4). Similarly, in **Thompson**, the section titled "The futility of reform" (pp. 284–85) places the reinvention lab case study in the context of past attempts at administrative reform, drawing attention to reasons for past failures in a way that emphasizes the significance of the successes of the reinvention lab program.

Stein's definition also points to the case study approach's tendency toward a pluralistic perspective on the complexity of causal relationships. Typically, case studies do not claim to have identified linear (or even multilinear) cause-effect relationships. They most often assume complex and reciprocal relationships among factors affecting outcomes. One of the prominent themes of **Johnston and Romzek** is the complexities involved in contract management (cf. p. 386, Figure 1). **Thompson** also explicitly discusses the "complex causal model" (p. 289) suggested by his examination of the reinvention lab program.

A weakness in Stein's definition is its focus on decision making, which is only one kind of phenomenon around which a case study might be built. Case studies can be focused on a wide variety of phenomena, including such things as a program, event, activity, process, individual, group of individuals, or organization. As was mentioned in the previous chapter, case studies that attend to the culture of a group or organization may be ethnographic. **Johnston and Romzek**'s study does focus on a kind of decision (a contract), but **Thompson** focuses on a federal program—a complex set of decisions, processes, and organizational actions.

R.K. Yin has offered this definition:

A case study is an empirical inquiry that

- investigates a contemporary phenomenon within its real-life context; when
- the boundaries between phenomenon and context are not clearly evident; and in which
- multiple sources of evidence are used. (1989, p. 23)

Yin helps us by pointing to the contemporary character of the phenomena addressed in the case studies, thus distinguishing case studies from histories. Again, the two case study examples provide evidence consistent with this definition. Both deal with contemporary phenomena. **Thompson** began his research on the reinvention labs in the same year (1993) that the program was launched, as did **Johnston and Romzek** (1997).

Like Stein, Yin also points to this research approach's attention to context, but he takes us a step further by addressing the natural, real-life setting aspect of case studies. Moreover, his definition highlights a significant challenge faced by anyone doing a case study—defining the limits of the study—when he points out that the boundaries between phenomenon and context are not obvious.

Although both examples do a fine job of placing boundaries around their cases, there is evidence that they faced some challenges in identifying and staying within them. **Thompson** addresses the challenge fairly directly in his explanations of how he decided which labs to include. He notes the heterogeneity of the activities that were officially designated as labs (p. 285) and comments in a note on the difficulty of being accurate regarding how many labs there were (p. 292, note 3). He also justifies his limiting the labs considered in his study to those "relating to the host agency's 'core task'" (p. 285). Moreover, I think the difficulty of staying within the boundaries of the case is further implied in **Thompson** in relation to one of the major theoretical propositions that he takes from March (1981)—the idea that reform is more likely to be successful when it amplifies "the force of natural organizational processes" (p. 290). Distinguishing between the impacts of a specific reform and impacts deriving from the momentum of natural organizational processes is a tremendous intellectual challenge. **Johnston and Romzek** do not explicitly address the difficulties they faced in identifying the parameters of their case, but they can be inferred from instances when the authors address contextual matters in order to explain what happened in the case. There are several instances of this. One deals with the way the Medicaid contract was influenced by problems deriving from the high cost of skilled nursing facility (SNF) care (pp. 384–85). Another involves the way difficulties with other contracts (e.g., the Children's Health Insurance Program) affected the Medicaid contract (p. 390). In their "Notes" they also discuss in-home health care, "although direct-care services are not a primary focus of our study" (p. 396, note 4).

Yin also explicitly addresses one of the "signature" aspects of case studies, the utilization of multiple sources of information. This aspect of case studies will be elaborated upon later in the section on data collection and generation, so at this point I will simply note that it is an important and common feature of case study approaches.

Examining a third and final attempt at defining what a case study is, we find that R.E. Stake does not even see the case study as a research method. He writes: "Case study is not a methodological choice but a choice of what is to be studied" (2003, p. 134). This derives in part from the tendency to use multiple information sources. As I mentioned earlier, it is also true that case studies can employ both qualitative and quantitative research approaches. Stake describes a case in the following terms:

- a functioning specific (e.g., a program, event, activity, process, individual, group of individuals, or organization)
- a bounded system (e.g., by time, activity, or place)
- an integrated system (structured, coherent, patterned behavior, a collection of related elements constituting a "self")

Stake's definition reiterates some points already made, but in focusing on the phenomenon being studied, his definition emphasizes the need to identify a specific thing to study and recognizes the variety of things that might be thus studied (2003). As mentioned earlier, the **Johnston and Romzek** case focuses upon a specific contract established to implement a program, and **Thompson** focuses on a collection of programs that represent an integrated part of a general reform effort. Like Stein and Yin, Stake also defines case study in a way that addresses the intellectual challenge of putting boundaries around what is studied.

More important, Stake's definition brings into view another intellectual challenge that is often faced in case studies—identifying the integrating aspects of the case that give it an identity. **Johnston and Romzek** found their integrating aspect in the Medicaid contract. **Thompson** is a good example of a more complex "functioning specific." It, therefore, provides a model for how to deal with this challenge, and his response to it is most directly addressed in the first two paragraphs of his "Methods" section (p. 285). When you read those paragraphs, please note how clearly he has delineated his primary unit of analysis, the second level of embedded units, and a third layer of embedded units. Also note the importance of an innovation's relationship to the host agency's "core task" in identifying whether it should be included in this study.

As you can see, defining the case study approach is no simple task. It is possible to identify certain family resemblances among case studies— things like addressing a contemporary phenomenon, focusing on an integrated system, attention to context, and recognition of complex causal patterns—but there is no single definition of the case study approach that is generally accepted.

## Kinds of Case Studies

Not only is there no single definition of the case study approach, there are also several kinds of case studies. Stake distinguishes three types of case study: intrinsic, instrumental, and collective (2003). When the purpose of the author is simply to examine the particular case, not to learn from it about some problem in general, Stake calls that an intrinsic case study. When the purpose is to learn about something else, he calls it an instrumental case study. When the author tells us about more than one case in trying to help us learn about something else, Stake calls that a collective case study.

Both **Johnston and Romzek** and **Thompson** are instrumental case studies. **Thompson** uses the reinvention labs to learn more about organizational reform. **Johnston and Romzek** use an example of contracting out for Medicaid case management services to explore the management complications involved in contracting out for social services. In using more than one case, **Thompson** might also be seen as representing a collective case study, but he sees it as another kind—one described by Yin.

Yin (1989, p. 46) distinguishes four basic types of case study by looking at several key aspects: single case designs, multiple case designs, holistic (single unit analysis), and embedded (multiple units of analysis). **Thompson** explicitly references Yin in describing his study:

> This study is representative of the single, embedded case study described by Yin (1989). The reinvention lab program itself represents the primary unit of analysis; the individual reinvention labs represent embedded units of analysis; and specific changes or proposed changes labeled "innovations" are further embedded within the individual laboratories. (p. 285)

**Johnston and Romzek** make no reference to case study designs in their article, but their article clearly fits Yin's single case, holistic design.

Yin also suggests that there are several different purposes that these types of case study might pursue: exploration, description, and explanation. In Yin's view, exploratory case studies are aimed at preparing the researcher for a later study that may or may not be a case study. A descriptive case study simply aims for an effective description of a phenomenon, but it does not attempt to address the causal relationships upon which an explanatory case study focuses (Yin 1993, p. 5). **Johnston and Romzek** describe their study as exploratory but provide no indication that it is aimed at preparing them for a later study. I would classify their article as explanatory because it examines how well theories of contracting and theories of accountability explain what happened in the case. I also interpret their article as implying that the explanation of this case holds more general lessons about contracting for social services.

J.L. Jensen and R. Rodgers offer another case study typology that includes snapshot, longitudinal, pre-post, patchwork, and comparative to the list of types of case study (2001, pp. 237–39). A snapshot case study looks at a single case at a single point in time. A longitudinal case study usually looks at the dynamics of change over time and, therefore, follows a case over a period of time. A pre-post case study looks at a case at two different points in time, usually before and after some intervention in order to address the impacts of the intervention. A patchwork case study integrates several studies of the same case in order to obtain a longitudinal perspective. Finally, a comparative case study looks at multiple cases in order to gain perspective from the comparison and/ or contrasts among them. **Johnston and Romzek**'s article seems to represent a longitudinal case study, but the period of time is rather short. They conducted three sets of interviews over a two-year period (p. 389, col. 2, par. 2). Still, their analysis addresses dynamics over time. **Thompson**'s work also seems to fit the longitudinal category since it involves three phases covering the period from 1993 to 1998 and examines the concept of "success" in a way that requires the passage of time, especially in the indicators "in place after three years" and "replication" (p. 286, Table 1).

The snapshot way of doing a single case study may be what most people think of when they consider case study approaches, but it clearly is not the only available design. Richness of detail is its distinguishing feature, but perspective can be added in other ways. For example, layers can be distinguished, and each layer given its own special attention (the embedded design). The time dimension can be expanded, or multiplied (i.e., multiple snapshots). Multiple cases can also be included in a study to provide 1) support for generalizing from the study, 2) a comparative basis, or 3) an informative contrast. The purpose of your study and the

---

**Box 5.2    Case Study Design Challenges**

**Identifying your case**

- identify the general topic(s) to which the case relates
- establish your research purpose
- articulate your research question

**Justifying your case study**

- explain why a case study approach is appropriate for this research project
- explain why this specific case (or cases) is (are) well-suited for this project

**Framing the case study**

- identify the integrating aspect
- identify the parameters
- construct an analytical framework

---

resources available to you are likely to be critical in deciding which kind of case study is most appropriate for you to pursue.

**Case Study Design Issues**

Designing a case study is essentially an intellectual challenge. It involves identifying a case to study, justifying that selection, and anticipating the logistical challenges that will likely be encountered. These facets of designing a case study are not always addressed in the same order. Most likely you will find yourself revisiting each of the facets, or at least parts of them, many times during your work on a case study research project (see Box 5.2).

One of the design issues that should be addressed fairly early is the question: Why use a case study approach (see Box 5.3)? Too often the answer appears to be that the researcher thinks it will be convenient to do a study of the agency for which he or she works. That is not a sufficient reason for doing a case study, but is also not a reason for deciding against a case study research project. Since scientific detachment would detract from the value of a qualitative case study approach, having relationships with the people being studied is desirable. But more on this later.

The place to begin consideration of whether to utilize a case study ap-

---

**Box 5.3   Reasons for Using a Qualitative Case Study Approach**

- To study a phenomenon in its natural, real-life context
- To focus on the special characteristics of the phenomenon being studied
- To report on a noteworthy success (or failure)
- To recognize the importance of the context surrounding the phenomenon being studied
- To explore the relationships among personal, collective, organizational, and structural dynamics
- To assist in theory development

---

proach is the same place to begin in considering any research design. You need to be quite clear about your research purpose and the general research question being asked. One way of clarifying your research purpose is to consider the more general topic(s) to which it relates. If you know the general topic and can identify the more specific purpose you will pursue, you can more easily explain to others what you are doing and why they might be interested. You also will have an easier time doing a literature review. The general topic will help you find literature. Your more specific research purpose will help you decide on what part of that literature to focus.

**Johnston and Romzek** and **Thompson** both address the general topic of administrative reform. Within that topic, **Johnston and Romzek** pursue a purpose related to contracting and accountability. **Thompson** is interested in understanding more about how reforms succeed.

Some research purposes are better suited to qualitative case study research than others. Quantitative approaches are well suited for testing hypotheses and predicting which factors influence an outcome. Qualitative case studies are better suited for exploring poorly understood topics and understanding complex relationships. For example, **Johnston and Romzek** describe their article as

> exploring the administrative and accountability dynamics that arise during the implementation of a reform—a reform based on the rhetoric of privatization, but which does not meet the conditions necessary to tap into market relationships. (p. 384)

**Thompson** indicates that his research was aimed at understanding "how reform has affected the day-to-day activities of front line federal employees" (p. 284).

With regard to research questions, Yin (1989) says that exploratory "what" questions can be addressed using a wide variety of research approaches, including case studies. For example, one might use a case study of the *Challenger* accident to explore what kinds of difficulties are faced in multi-organizational collaborations (cf. Romzek and Dubnick 1987). The two kinds of questions Yin thinks are better suited for case study research are *how* (descriptive or explanatory) and *why* (explanatory). As the previous quote from **Thompson** indicates, he was pursuing a descriptive *how* question. Among the research questions that **Johnston and Romzek** pursued is the explanatory question: *Why* did the cost-savings that are often associated with contracting out not materialize when Kansas contracted out for social services?

You might also choose to do a case study based upon the special characteristics of the specific case you are considering. So, a key question may be: why study *this* case? If your interest in studying the case is more than simple convenience, it may well be that you genuinely believe that the focus of your study offers a learning opportunity. Perhaps you think that the case represents an interesting experience from which others could learn. As noted above, the impetus for doing a case study is often that a phenomenon grabs the interest of the researcher. The phenomenon might not have been thought of as a research problem until the researcher was looking for one, but that in itself should not be sufficient reason for deciding against doing the case study. A case is frequently selected for study because it is seen as a noteworthy success or failure. It may also be selected because it can help us better understand a dynamic (or complex of dynamics) that is important to the field.

In explaining why they chose to focus on the Kansas case, **Johnston and Romzek** explain that "the State of Kansas has taken a national lead in privatizing certain social services" (p. 384). They also suggest there are a number of ways the case might help us understand something important about the political and administrative dynamics of contracting out for social services, especially "contracting in a non-market environment" (p. 395). Their article reports on a noteworthy failure.

**Thompson**, on the other hand, offers an example of a noteworthy success. In explaining why he chose the reinvention labs case, he offers multiple reasons. He describes it as "a useful opportunity to reexamine the construct of administrative reform" (p. 284). He finds the exceptional qualities of the reinvention labs reason for attending to them (pp. 284–85), and connects those qualities to the explanation of how this reform resulted in success, representing a counterexample to the general trend in the literature to see reform as futile.

Specific characteristics of the case study approach may also help to decide whether it is a good one for the research project you are considering. Both **Johnston and Romzek** and **Thompson** studied a phenomenon in its natural setting. Often, qualitative researchers engage over a period of time with the participants involved in the phenomenon they are studying. Johnston, through her work for the Rockefeller Institute's State Capacity Study, has apparently been involved in field studies of the actors in the Kansas State case for some time (p. 395, col. 2, par. 3). Similarly, Thompson indicates that his article derives from a broader study that has taken place over five years (pp. 285 and 286).

Having identified a case study, you will need to begin to delineate it. One aspect of that delineation involves focusing on its special characteristics, and another aspect involves attending to its context. That takes us back to part of Stake's definition, his description of a case as an integrated system composed of structured, coherent, patterned behavior—a collection of related elements constituting a "self." As Stake notes, to say that something is an integrated system is not to claim that the system works well. It may be working very badly, but if it has its own unique life with relationships and patterned dynamics, if it has a coherence, then it can qualify as an integrated system (2003). The integrating aspect may emerge from the case, it may be created by the researcher's perspective, or it may be that the researcher's perspective is a kind of recognition of the system's integrity. When a policy initiative is put forth, it may create what Fox and Miller (1996) described as an "energy field" that gives direction (or at least impetus) to the interactions among the network of people and organizations involved in implementing and evaluating that initiative. As was mentioned earlier, the central integrating aspect in **Thompson** had to do with reinvention lab innovations relating to the "core task" of their host agency (p. 285, col. 2, par. 3). **Johnston and Romzek** examined an energy field that was integrated around a specific contract for Medicaid case management services.

Once the case is selected and its integrating aspect identified, it needs to be placed within some parameters—i.e., you need to decide what is not integral to the account you are constructing of the case. You need to attend carefully to what is in the case and what is part of its context. Otherwise, your project may expand so much that it becomes impractical. You may think that studying a specific agency provides you with sufficiently tight focus that you do not need to think much about putting limits around it; but even if you are focusing on a given agency, its work involves relationships with many other agencies and organizations and you will need to place limits on how much you address about those relationships and the actions of those other organizations. You may also need to decide upon a time frame.

Since the challenges in delineating boundaries faced by the authors of the two exemplar articles have already been addressed in relation to defining the case study approach, I will not repeat that here. Instead, let me take an example from my own work. In my case study of Spokane's solid waste policymaking (L. Luton 1996), it was clear that related (and some very interesting) developments would continue to occur for a number of years. I had to decide at what point in time my treatment of the case would end. That decision was aided by my publication schedule. I also had to decide how much history to include. That was a more challenging decision. My general tendency is to see everything as related to everything else, so I had to decide what to include, and what not to include, based on how important it was in the dynamics of the case as I understood it. Such boundaries are both fuzzy and permeable; they may represent one of the more difficult intellectual challenges you face in doing a case study. Deciding where those parameters were was the most difficult part of that case study project. Do not be dismayed if you need to modify where you place the parameters as your understanding of the case evolves.

If the researcher has identified what is core and what is periphery, a case study approach can be an excellent way of examining dynamics within the case and between the case and its context. **Thompson** demonstrates quite well how a case study explores personal, collective, organizational, and structural dynamics. He specifically addresses the impact of Joe Thompson (pp. 287–88), discusses a failed attempt to organize self-directed teams (p. 288), criticizes the organizational processes that led to delay and impersonal treatment (p. 287), and examines the impact of the organizational split between the Veterans Services Division and the Adjudication Division (pp. 287–88).

Case studies have also been used frequently to develop theory. **Johnston and Romzek** do a meticulous job of comparing the ability of different theories of contracting and accountability to explain what happened in their case. Similarly, **Thompson** examines the ability of different theories of organizational change to predict whether reforms will result in success.

Further discussion of theory development would take us into development and use of an analytical framework, and that will come a bit later in this chapter. Next I will address some of the logistical issues involved in doing a case study.

## Logistical Issues

Some logistical issues need to be considered before investing significant time and effort in a case study research project. They involve making sure that you can gain access to the people and data necessary for successful completion of your case study research project and whether you have the resources you will need to complete it (see Box 5.4).

First, let's address the issue of access to people and data. If one of your reasons for selecting a case for study is convenience, access to the data and people needed for the project may not be an issue. If you do not already have an avenue for such access, this is something you will need to address very early in the work on your project. When I decided to write my book on solid waste policymaking in Spokane, I already had good relationships with local government officials and their consultants because of other work I had done in the community as a professor of public administration. I also had good relations with citizens' groups because I had been involved in a neighborhood group that formed to address concerns about a study that identified a potential ash landfill site in our area. This is an aspect of case study reporting that needs to be improved in our field. Very seldom do we include much information about how we developed the relationships that were needed in order to gain sufficient access.[3] **Thompson** does not report much about gaining access in his article, but it is clear that considerable groundwork was laid in order to be able to interview 64 people at 19 labs over a five-year period. In addition, he obtained access to archival materials (p. 285). **Johnston and Romzek** also report little about what they did to obtain access, but they conducted 37 interviews over a two-year period and were allowed to access some administrative documents (p. 389).

Another consideration is whether you have (or can obtain) the time and financial resources you will need to complete the project. Generally,

> **Box 5.4 Logistical Challenges in Doing a Case Study**
> **What are the data sources I need to access/create?**
> - files and organizational documents?
> - interviews?
> - other reports?
> - newspaper articles or other news media accounts?
>
> **Who are the people from whom I need assistance/ information?**
> - government officials?
> - consultants?
> - activists in community organizations?
> - interest group activists?
> - people in the media?
>
> **Do I have a way of gaining access to them?**
> - already established relationships?
> - friends, acquaintances, colleagues, contacts who can help me access them?
> - reason to believe they will be willing to assist me?

it takes longer to do a case study than to do research based on statistical analysis of an existing database—or even of a survey designed and run specifically for your research project. Both examples used throughout this chapter involved years of research. They probably also entailed significant expenses related to conducting the interviews, but case study research may be less expensive than survey research, depending on the costs associated with gathering documents, going to meetings, interviewing, etc., and recording and managing the information thus gathered.

**Collecting and Creating Data**

As was mentioned earlier, one of the definitional features of case study research approaches is utilization of multiple sources of information. This feature also distinguishes the case study approach quite clearly from many other approaches. For example, survey research typically utilizes only data gathered through distribution of a survey instrument.

Many quantitative analyses depend on data from a single database, one that may or may not have been created for the purposes of the research project. Similarly, qualitative interviewing and narrative inquiry are often limited to or focused upon a single way of gathering information. The value of the research, consequently, depends highly on the quality of the single approach. Ethnographic research may well involve more than field observations, and case study research typically involves collecting data from a variety of kinds of sources—interviews, field research, and document analysis, for example.

In using multiple sources of information, case study research is not so dependent upon a single source and may have the ability to verify the accuracy of its sources by checking them against each other. This cross-checking for accuracy through the use of multiple sources of information is sometimes referred to as triangulation. As T.A. Schwandt explains, the purpose of triangulation "is to examine a conclusion (assertion, claim, etc.) from more than one vantage point" (2001, p. 257) in order to assess the degree of confidence we should have regarding it.

The sources of evidence commonly utilized in public administration case study research can be classified into six basic types: (1) organizational documents, (2) organizational files, (3) interviews, (4) observation, (5) media reports, and (6) other studies related to the case or its context (see Box 5.5). Because previous chapters addressed interviews and observation, in this chapter I will focus on dealing with data that derive from reading documents, files, reports, and other studies.

Organizational documents include such things as letters, emails, Web sites (and other Internet-facilitated communications such as blogs and chat rooms), memoranda, newsletters, announcements, meeting agendas, meeting minutes, annual reports, other written reports (including working papers and consultant reports), organizational charts, requests for proposals, proposals, and press releases. In addition to being the source of some of the items listed under organizational documents, organizational files may include such things as budget and personnel data. The reason that I distinguish organizational files from organizational documents is that, because they may contain more sensitive information, they are often not available under the Freedom of Information Act or similar state statutes. Gaining access to them may well be a significantly greater challenge.

If you use media reports as one of your sources of data, you need recognize that the quality of the information is highly dependent upon the quality of the reporter, the general editorial perspective of the media organization, and the structural dynamics of the news media business. Some reporters have more experience and/or expertise in understanding the events they cover than others. The general editorial perspective of the media organization may also influence such things as the kinds of reporters they hire, the amount of space or time given to a story, and even the "angle" that the reporter will use to frame the story. The structural dynamics of the news media business include factors such as the profit motive and corporate agendas that may also influence media reports.

Still, media reports may be a crucial source for information in a case study. If it were not for the media, we would know much less about the operations of government. For most of us their coverage influences our understanding of the context of the specific case study we research. There may even be a way in which the media's coverage of a specific issue has a more direct bearing on our understanding of it. For example, because of the quality of her work, in my case study of Spokane's solid waste policymaking I relied quite a bit on the reporting of a local newspaper journalist, Karen Dorn Steele. Her specialty for the paper was environmental reporting, and she was generally given considerable leeway by the paper to spend much time developing stories prior to publishing them. She understood what she was reporting on, but she also had a personal perspective that was more aligned with environmental interest groups than with corporate interests. I had to factor in my respect for her expertise and my understanding of her perspective as I decided how to incorporate her reports into my case study.

The work of other researchers may also be valuable sources of information for your case study. Their work may be available at professional conferences, through professional journals, or as publications of consulting firms or think tanks (in hard copy from their offices or as electronic documents on their Web sites). Fortunately for public administration researchers, much of the work of other researchers (having been publicly funded) results in public documents, but when reports are done for limited distribution, you may need to borrow a copy from a contact you make in the course of your research project. The main "filters" you should apply to these reports derive from recognition of their original purpose and the client for which the research was done. The purpose and/or the client may influence the content in a way that needs to be attended to in assessing the utility of the report for your research.

In his section on methods, **Thompson** specifically mentions semi-structured interviews and archival materials, but he seems also to have

---

**Box 5.5    Common Sources of Data for Case Studies**

- organizational documents
- organizational files
- interviews
- observation
- media reports
- other studies related to the case or its context

---

used at least one elite interview (see Kamensky in "References" on p. 292), a videotape (*Heroes of Reinvention* in "References" on p. 292), organizational documents (U.S. Federal Supply Service 1997) and observation (for example, in following the career advancement of Joe Thompson [p. 288]). In their methodology section, **Johnston and Romzek** say they used semistructured interviews of two groups of officials and an elected official. They also reviewed administrative and legislative documents (p. 389). Their references and notes sections provide evidence that they also used media accounts (e.g., p. 396, notes 1 and 3).

Other research texts provide considerable guidance on ways to organize your data. (See the "Recommended Readings" list at the end of this chapter for some good examples.) I find that each researcher needs to develop his or her own way, so I will not elaborate here on ways to organize your data, but will limit myself to some basic suggestions on the topic.

You will probably want to develop multiple, but coordinated, ways of organizing your data. The information from each of the different sources will take different shapes. Interviews may lead to transcripts that will need to be organized in ways that relate to the persons interviewed. The contents of those transcripts may need to be coded based on such things as questions asked, topics, issues or themes to which they relate, and the place they are likely to appear in your project report. (For more on this see Chapter 2.) Similarly, field observations are often organized in several manners: according to the dates and/or places they were made; by the topics, issues, or themes to which they relate; and by the places in which they are likely to appear in your project report. (See Chapter 4.) Organizational documents, organizational files, and other reports often are first organized as if they were in a small library—by author, title, and/ or topic. You will also need to develop some way of retrieving specific aspects of their contents based on the issues or themes you decide to address. Researchers often keep media reports in a "news clippings" file that is organized by the date of the report, but you will need to supplement that with some way of indicating the topics, issues, or themes to which they relate. You probably will also need to take notes on your thoughts or reflections about the contents of all the data you collect or create; these thoughts and reflections will also need to be organized, perhaps based on the same issues or themes. The basic idea is to organize your data so that it can be retrieved as needed in thinking through and writing up your report.

Finally, it is an important part of the qualitative research tradition to recognize that when you collect, create and organize data, you are acting as an active agent, not simply receiving or recognizing the data that is "out there." As Morse and Richards point out, "It helps to think of qualitative data as *made* rather than merely 'collected'" (2002, p. 87, emphasis in the original). It may be easier to see the creative aspect of data gathering in relation to interviewing and observation than it is in relation to reading various kinds of documents, but documents require interpretation and interpretation involves creativity. Certainly, by the time you are organizing your data, you are transforming it to suit your own purposes, but that is also the case as you decide what to collect— what is relevant, important, or interesting. Because you cannot collect everything, selection is necessary. Although this introduces a potential place for improper bias to enter your work, if you are conscientious in your work and honest with your readers about how you did it, that should not be a problem.

### Analyzing It

I agree with Stake that "there is no particular moment when data analysis begins" (1995, p. 71). As soon as a researcher identifies a case as "interesting," he or she has some idea about what the case means, represents, or provides some guidance on or insight into. That moment may well have taken place long before the idea to do a case study was born. For this reason it is important to record your thoughts, feelings, and insights throughout your work on the case study. People have many ways of doing that, but the most important thing is to do it. Whether you dictate your thoughts into some kind of recorder, scribble notes on index cards or a notebook (or napkins or whatever piece of paper is within reach at the time), or set aside a time to journal each day, recording your ideas throughout the time that you work on your case study will enhance the quality of your work significantly.

Those original notes or recordings represent your earliest steps in analyzing the case study. When you begin to organize them and your data, you enter a higher-level stage of analysis. Organizing your data and your reflections, even if it is simply placing them into categories, requires you to look at them in a different way. Why does *this* data belong in *that* category? Some qualitative researchers refer to this as moving or thinking "up" from the data. Morse and Richards (2002) describe it as "abstracting" (moving from the specific to the more general). J.W. Creswell (1998, p. 143) depicts the process as an upward spiral, a visual image that evokes the circular and recursive aspect of analysis, but the orderly spiral does not quite do justice to the messiness of the experience. Moving up actually involves moving back and forth between the data and analytical concepts in some way that eventually leads to "upward" motion. The various vehicles for moving up from the data include categorization (including reducing, sorting, organizing, comparing, and contrasting), conceptualization, hypothesis generation, proposition development, argument construction, and metaphor generation. Finding what works for you will be a very individualized experience. As Creswell has said, "Data analysis is not off-the-shelf; rather it is custom-built, revised and choreographed" (1998, p. 142).

In building and rebuilding your data organizing system, you are already into your work on analyzing the case study. To categorize something as relevant to a topic, as important for a purpose, or as interesting for a reason, is to begin analyzing the relationship between parts of what you see and the more general picture in which it fits. To place bits of information so that they help to identify patterns, recognize similarities, construct meaningful connections, is to interpret and analyze—to facilitate understanding.

When the time comes to focus upon analysis of the data, there are three crucial steps to include: (1) reimmerse yourself in the data, (2) rethink your categories, and (3) place it all in an analytical framework. It is important to go back through your data thoroughly and thoughtfully. You may be surprised at the new insights that you gain by doing so. Reviewing and rethinking your categories at this stage is also important. The new overview you get may lead to ideas about new categories and/or new ways to combine previously identified categories. One of the things that may

---

**Box 5.6    Analysis Activities**

**Examining the data**
- immerse and reimmerse yourself in the data
- think and rethink about the data
- analyze and reanalyze the data and your notes/thoughts about it

**"Moving up" from the data**
- categorize the data
- reduce the data
- sort the data
- organize the data
- compare the data
- contrast the data
- conceptualize the data

**Making meaning**
- interpret the data
- construct patterns
- form propositions
- mount arguments
- generate metaphors

---

facilitate the rethinking of your categories is the conscientious use of an analytical framework. You may have had one in mind earlier, or, if you are working from a grounded theory approach, you may only now be ready to see what framework emerges from the data. In either case, in order to address the general meaning of case studies, it helps to have some sort of framework; this is the time to make sure that you have one that serves your purposes.

Your analytical framework should be clearly related to your general research topic, your specific research purpose, and your research question(s). An analytical framework provides a basis for examining patterns and deriving meaning, a basis for organizing what is observed and (perhaps) for predicting what previous research or a particular theoretical perspective suggests should be observed (see Box 5.6). How close does the case's pattern fit with the predicted pattern? Some case studies include more than one analytical framework to provide an opportunity for comparison. Is one of the frameworks more consistent with what was seen?

Both **Johnston and Romzek** and **Thompson** were organized around analytical frameworks designed to gain insight into the dynamics of the cases they studied. **Johnston and Romzek** specifically address theoretical frameworks related to contracting and accountability (pp. 385–89), comparing the market model that emphasizes the benefits deriving from competition to an alternative model by Kettl that emphasizes the need for public managers to become smart buyers in a situation where there is limited competition. They conclude that "the state's decision to privatize case management services for elderly Medicaid recipients does not conform to the market model of contracting and privatization" (p. 390), and find that the Kansas case is more accurately described by the Kettle model (p. 391). **Thompson** utilizes March's theoretical framework, which says that reform is more likely to be successful if it amplifies an organization's "natural" processes of innovation and change (p. 285, col. 1, par. 2). In his interpretation, the reinvention labs enhanced their prospects for change by doing what March's framework suggests.

Stake (1995) emphasizes the connection between analysis and interpretation and identifies two basic strategies—categorical aggregation and direct interpretation—*both* of which are used in case studies. In categorical aggregation, you compile descriptions of instances to create a more general picture. In direct interpretation, you tease out the meaning of a single episode or instance with no need for aggregation of instances to arrive at a more general meaning. **Johnston and Romzek** utilize direct interpretation. They directly interpret a single instance to provide evidence supporting a claim that there was little or no market competition in the dynamics surrounding contracting for case management services. Included as evidence in the instance are vigorous lobbying by the group that won the contract (p. 389) and consideration by the state of only one contractor (p. 390). **Thompson** uses categorical aggregation. He looks at 19 labs and 26 separate innovations to aggregate support for March's theory regarding how best to achieve successful reform (p. 285).

Within both of those strategies, the researcher will likely engage in pattern construction and/or naturalistic generalization. In pattern construction, you look for correspondence between expected or predicted patterns and the ones observed (what Yin called "pattern matching logic").

**Johnston and Romzek** describe a pattern in the Kansas case that fits better with Kettl's model for contracting out services. The pattern in **Thompson** is a bit more complex, involving solicitation of the lab designation, multiple indicators for "success," and adoption of innovations by other units (p. 289); but it, too, involves looking for correspondence between expected patterns and the ones observed.

Stake describes naturalistic generalizations as "conclusions arrived at through personal engagement in life's affairs or by vicarious experience so well constructed that the person feels as if it happened to themselves" (1995, p. 85). This kind of meaning making is important both for the researcher and the reader of the research report, and the ability to describe a case so that it presents the potential for a vicarious sense of it is a crucial skill for a case study researcher. Although one can only reach this conclusion by interpretation, I think **Johnston and Romzek** assume that their readers will see enough in their case to adopt a similar explanation for their own experience with problematic attempts at contracting for social services. Evidence supporting this interpretation is found throughout their introductory paragraphs and in their conclusion in such sentences as: "All too frequently, political rhetoric characterizes privatization as a preferable alternative to public provision regardless of whether market rationales for privatization exist" (p. 394). **Thompson**, on the other hand, is more focused on persuading us to alter our concept of administrative reform (p. 291).

### Analyzing Documents as Actors

Analysis in case study research is quite complex because of the multiple kinds of data being examined and the dual perspective that is likely to be involved. If you were only examining interviews, observations, and documents for themes, that task would be complex enough, but in case study research the meaning of the content of documents is not all that is relevant. How those documents affected the dynamics of the case study is also important. Moreover, a case study project is not only likely to involve analysis of more than one document but of multiple kinds of documents.

The chapters on interviewing, narrative inquiry, and ethnography addressed data collection and analysis in terms of finding content-related meaning. Here I will address another aspect of document analysis that is likely to be relevant in case study research—the idea that documents are not only texts; they are also agents or actors. They are produced, exist, and have impacts in a network of actors, which "generates questions

---

**Box 5.7   Questions to Ask About Documents as Actors**

- Who produced this document?
- Who was the intended audience?
- Who else attended to it?
- What was the intended impact?
- What impact did it have on other actors?
- What impact did it have on the dynamics of the case?
- How was that impact accomplished?

---

about what documents 'do,' [as well as] . . . what they 'say'" (L. Prior 2008, p. 112). Documents "not only have a certain 'meaning,' they also have force, that is, they are not only about things, they also do things" (L.A. Word and R.O. Kroger 2000, p. 4) (see Box 5.7).

One way that documents have impact is a function of their content, so I do not mean to suggest that the impacts of documents as actors in a case study's dynamics is divorced from the meaning(s) obtained by interpreting their content. In that sense, a rhetorical analysis such as was done by Feldman et al. (2004; see exemplar articles in Chapter 3) might be quite useful in interpreting documents collected as part of a case study. Chapters 2, 3, and 4 cover ways of analyzing data collected in interviews, which might also prove useful. When looking at the content to better understand a document's impact, one might focus on "what themes, frames, and discourse are being presented" (D. Altheide et al. 2008, p. 130). In addition, one might ask what is being emphasized and what is being discounted by the ways the documents are organized. The examination of content in analyzing what the documents "did" would concern how those themes, frames, etc., influenced the impact of the documents on what happened in the case study.

In their role as actors, it is appropriate to ask of documents: Who produced this (a news media organization, government agency, interest group)? Who was the intended audience (relevant publics, clients, legislators, agency administrators)? Who else became part of the audience? What was its intended impact or communication purpose (e.g., information, description, explanation, advocacy)? What impact did it have on others or on the dynamics involved in the case study? How was it accomplished?

F. Fischer and J. Forester (1993) present a view of policy analysis that is helpful in analyzing the impacts of documents as actors influencing the dynamics of the case study. They suggest that a policy argument involves both analytic content and practical performance. The practical performance aspect includes networking, bargaining, and persuading. In addition to recognizing that documents have impacts on policymaking, they suggest that the activities involved in producing the document should be examined. Was the document created by "bureaucratically institutionalized policy procedures" (1993, p. 9)? If so, in what ways did those procedures affect the content? If not, what were the procedures that were involved in its creation and how did they affect the content? What strategy was involved? What coalition did it help (or hinder)? Whose concerns were included, and whose were ignored?

In my case study of solid waste policymaking in Spokane, Washington, I discussed the impacts of documents in at least a couple of ways. First, I examined the impacts of two documents that were produced to influence the outcome of a city election—an election that turned on public attitudes toward a proposed waste-to-energy incinerator (1996, pp. 18–20). The first document, "Risking Spokane," analyzed the potential ill effects of that incinerator; it was produced by opponents of the incinerator and distributed to 25,000 Spokane households. The second document, "Waste-to-Energy Works," was produced by an interest group that favored the incinerator, and would never have existed but for the impact its sponsors saw "Risking Spokane" having on the outcome of the election and the decision to proceed with the incinerator. Second, I devoted a chapter to analyzing the impact of the news media upon the dynamics of the case study. In that chapter, the institutions that produced the news coverage and their rather standardized tendency to present "the two sides" (when there are often more than just two) were examined.

Although it is not clear exactly how **Thompson** utilized the documents he says were a source of data (p. 285), there are passages where he shows that he saw documents as actors, as having an impact on the dynamics of his case studies. In his section on the New York Regional Office/Veterans Benefit Administration, he describes how changing the relationship of counselors with clients' files was central to the success of the reform. Changing the institutional process meant giving the counselors direct access to files and connecting those counselors to a specific list of clients for whom they were responsible. Also, when he discusses the larger issue of the National Performance Review and reinvention labs, he specifically notes the way that a letter from then-Vice President Al Gore became a source of legitimacy: "I would take out my letter from

Gore sanctioning our initiative" (p. 290). The letter from Gore impacted the acceptance of reinvention labs as change agents.

**Johnston and Romzek** explicitly focus upon the gap between the political rhetoric (often embodied in documents) and "the reality of the contracting experience" (p. 383). In their analysis, the rhetoric often influences people's perceptions of the dynamics of contracting out in a way that makes the "reality" more difficult to see and more difficult to manage. Instead of obtaining the benefits attributed to competition (greater efficiency and more innovation), the Kansas experience in contracting out for Medicaid services resulted in the transfer of monopoly from the government to private hands. "Under the rhetoric of privatization, the government has reduced the size of its most unpopular bureaucracy—the social services agency—by shifting responsibility for this service to a nonprofit interest group" (p. 395).

Analyzing documents as actors in the dynamics of case studies is a strategy that fits well with a pragmatic professional field such as public administration. We do need to understand the content meaning of documents, but for our field, this type of understanding is simply not enough; we also need to understand what impact documents have on what happens. How does the talk walk?

### Analysis as a Social Experience

As a qualitative case study researcher, you should realize that you are not the only one engaged in analyzing the case (or cases) you present. Your readers will also analyze your analysis. While your analysis may set a framework that influences theirs, they will conduct their own analyses of the case study, comparing it to their experiences and/or to other cases with which they are familiar. In other words, they participate actively in making the case transferable, rather than passively accepting the researcher's interpretation of the data. As they interpret the case's meaning for them, they expand its meaning beyond the unique case as it is presented. Your analysis is intended to facilitate other people's understanding, but it is not the final word.

Which takes us to the task you face in writing the case study.

### Writing It

When you write a case study, you write for two categories of people— an audience and yourself—but usually in the opposite order. When you begin composing your data and analysis into a written document, you probably will be writing for yourself. That is okay. Writing a case study continues the process of data creation and analysis. It is "a way of finding out about yourself and your topic" (L. Richardson 2003, p. 499). As you write, you continue to analyze your case; so, at least in the early stages, you are mostly making sense of it for yourself. That, of course, is necessary before you can help others make sense of it. At some point in the writing process, you can begin to attend more to your intended audience, at which point you focus more on presenting your analysis as clearly and effectively as possible.

There are several challenges to address in writing a case study: your relationship with your audience, compositional structure, compositional techniques, and your relationship with the participants.

### *Relationship with Your Audience*

Qualitative case studies recognize that the case study is not the case. It is an interpretation of the case. **Thompson**, for example, is very direct in describing his article as interpretation (e.g., in the abstract and p. 291). The researcher/writer is an interpreter, not a reporter, an active agent in creating an interpretation, not a transcriber of words representing "the facts of the case." This recognition of the creative role that you play as you research and write the case study does not relieve you of the burden of presenting the case as honestly as you can. It may even make that burden more difficult to carry because you are not able to rely on research protocols and standards for statistical analysis to convince your audience that you are presenting the case honestly, accurately, and with integrity.

There are, however, some steps you can use to enhance the credibility of your case study composition. First, you should be open about your presence and the role you play. This includes directly disclosing your situation in relation to the case. If the case is based on a specific organization, do you work in the organization? Are you a friend or a professional colleague of someone who does? If not, how did you gain access? What are your interpretive inclinations (biases, values, etc.)? Places that you might address such issues include the introduction, where you state your research purpose and present your research questions. Reflectively addressing why that purpose interested *you* and why those questions seemed important to *you,* rather than dealing with those items only in terms of why they are interesting and important to the profession, can help your credibility with readers. They know that researchers have personal reasons for the work they do. Telling them what your reasons are will show your honesty and help them to assess what you have to say, without needing to guess so much about such things.

You can also address your role in the composition when you address methodology. One of the traditions that has evolved in qualitative research is to think of the researcher as the "instrument." So it might be a good idea to include in the section on method a subsection on the role of the researcher. You are part of the method; therefore, you should be as transparent about who you are and what you did as possible. You should reveal the strategies you used to gain access, to gain the confidence of participants and informants, etc., to give readers a better idea of who you are. The levels and qualities of your research skills are also important. How did you learn to observe, interview, etc.? What did you do to make your procedures transparent and accountable?

Neither **Johnston and Romzek** nor **Thompson** do well on this aspect of qualitative research writing practices. Although they do not hide their long-term connections with the participants in their studies, they are not open and direct about discussing them. The reader is left to examine the article carefully to obtain what still remains a vague sense of the relationship between the authors and the participants.

### Compositional Structure

There is no standard compositional structure for a case study. The structure should reflect the researcher's understanding and facilitate readers' understanding. I find it helpful when working on the flow of the composition to keep in mind these two questions: (1) What do the readers need to know? (2) When do they need to know it? In order for readers to understand some things, they need previously to be introduced to others. In order for readers to understand what sense you make of the case, it may help to present aspects of the case in a particular order.

If you prefer to follow a prescribed compositional structure, a case study project might not be a good approach for you. "People who do not like to compose probably should not do case studies" (Yin 1989, p. 127). If you enjoy composing, a case study approach provides you an opportunity to be more flexible in structuring and writing your composition.

Yin (1989) identified six alternative compositional structures for case studies: linear-analytic, comparative, chronological, theory building, "suspense," and nonsequential structures. The linear-analytic is the traditional research report format—it follows the issue or problem, methods, findings, conclusions, and/or implications framework. Yin's comparative structure focuses on one case, repeating the case from alternative perspectives, thus comparing alternative descriptions or explanations. Sequences of events provide the framework for the chronological structure. Presentation of a theoretical argument guides the structure in the theory-building format. Ironically, the "suspense" structure entails starting with a direct "answer" regarding the outcome of a case and structuring the remainder of the composition as an explanation of that answer (perhaps with alternative answers addressed as part of that explanation, or after it). Finally, as the name implies, the nonsequential composition structure presents the case in sections, the order of which is not particularly important. If it is well constructed, a reader can begin with any section of the case study composition and jump around among the sections without diminishing its descriptive power.

The compositional structures of **Johnston and Romzek** and **Thompson** are most clearly examples of Yin's theory-building category, intending as they do to make cases for specific theoretical frameworks. They both also fit the linear-analytic structure quite nicely. Perhaps they realized that the *Public Administration Review* audience would be more easily persuaded if they followed the traditional format; or, they may simply have followed that format because it was one with which they were familiar and comfortable.

Probably the most common case study compositional structures used in public administration journals are the linear-analytic, chronological, and theory building. These general types also may be modified and/or combined in various ways. One way in which the linear-analytic structure may be altered to better fit the case study approach is in the literature review section. Sometimes that section is driven by the theory-building purpose of the case study, so it looks more like a primer on one or more theoretical perspectives than a literature review. The literature review section may also be replaced by a section that uses literature (or other sources) to present the historical context of the case.

### Compositional Techniques

Some people who write case studies have begun to reject traditional academic composition techniques.[4] However, none of these innovative authors, so far, has come from the field of public administration. You may decide to be among the first, but even if you do not take on that challenge, there are a few compositional technique issues that are so basic to qualitative case study approaches that you need to consider them carefully. One deals with presenting the "voice of the researcher." Second is the need to write an engaging account. Third is the challenge of providing the readers with a "feeling" for the case.

Compositional techniques that you can use to present the "voice of the researcher" and be open about your presence and role in the case include writing in first person, and adding personal, reflective notes—either as footnotes or endnotes. Few public administration case study authors have written in the first person. The traditional role of the researcher as "neutral expert" has quite a hold on the field, so it may be difficult to be comfortable with this technique. Even if you are comfortable with it, your peers (or manuscript reviewers) may not be. The qualitative research tradition includes a perspective that eschews the neutral expert tradition, but the field of public administration has not yet moved very far in that direction. On the other hand, public administration research practices do include the use of reflective and explanatory notes, so you may find this method easier to incorporate.

Writing an engaging account is a challenge faced to some degree in all qualitative research approaches, but because the case is so central to the case study approach, and because there is no standard compositional structure, it may be a good idea to structure your composition in a way that reflects the uniqueness of your case. As was mentioned earlier in this chapter, cases are often chosen by researchers simply because they found them interesting. When writing the case study composition, you need to present the case in a way that helps readers understand why you found it interesting. To some degree, based on the way they used their "rhetoric versus reality" framework to provide a catchy thread holding their argument together, **Johnston and Romzek** can be given credit for doing this. **Thompson**'s compositional technique is quite traditional.

If you want to engage readers in the case study, you cannot simply tell your audience *why* you found the case interesting. As is the situation for a writer of stories, you need to *show* them. You can do more telling as the author of a case study than you can as the author of a story, but be sure not to rely entirely on explanation or exhortation to do the trick. Ways of showing rather than telling include writing what Richardson called "evocative representations" (2003, p. 572)—perhaps character sketches and/or short stories about particular episodes. By *showing,* you let readers share in your sense that the case is interesting. Both **Johnston and Romzek** and **Thompson** rely on telling, not showing.

Because the value of a case study rests largely on the ability of the reader to gain a vivid sense of what happened, you also need to incorporate compositional techniques that give readers a feeling for the experience. One way this can be accomplished is through "thick description"—detailed, sensorially rich, observationally and experientially focused description. N.K. Denzin says thick description "presents detail, context, emotion, and the webs of social relationships. . . . The voices, feelings, actions, and meanings of interacting individuals are heard" (1989, p. 83). B.L. Berg adds these elements to the definition of thick description: It is aimed not only at drawing a detailed picture of events observed, actors involved, but also at describing the stated and "understood" rules influencing the actions and more general context in which they arise. It includes narration, analysis, and interpretation (2004, p. 181). At its best, it is characterized by coherence, elegance, and integrity. Neither **Johnston and Romzek** nor **Thompson** utilized thick description in their articles. (See Chapter 4, note 3, for examples of thick description.)

Other compositional techniques that can help readers gain a feeling of the case involve ways of presenting the voices of the participants. When you experienced the case, you experienced a multiplicity of voices. Not everything was presented to you from your perspective. In a well-composed case study, readers should also be given the chance to hear more than the writer's voice. A common way of doing this is to include direct quotations from the participants. Another way, and one that is very effective in presenting the multiplicity of voices as they relate to each other, is to include dialogue. I know of no journal article case studies in public administration that have made a serious effort to do this. **Johnston and Romzek** make little effort to give voice to the participants, simply attributing views to them (p. 390) or quoting one of them (p. 391). **Thompson**'s way of giving voice to participants is to make brief references to the way specific participants saw something, perhaps including a direct quote from them (e.g., pp. 287–89). (Chapters 2 and 3 address the compositional challenges involved in presenting others' voices in more detail.)

Unfortunately, journal article case studies in public administration have not yet begun to adopt nontraditional compositional techniques. This is an area where we could learn from other researchers and take greater advantage of the potential that qualitative approaches possess.

---

**Box 5.8    Writing Considerations**

**Making sense of the case**
- write to make sense for yourself
- write to make sense to others

**Your relationship with your audience**
- recognizing yourself as interpreter
- disclosing your perspective
- disclosing your role

**Compositional structure**
- flow
- alternative structures

**Compositional techniques**
- presenting your voice
- thick description
- presenting voices of the participants

**Relationships with participants**
- honoring promises (explicit and implicit) to them
- respecting them and their perspectives
- protecting vulnerable participants and/or agencies

---

*Relationship with Your Participants*

Giving voice to the participants is also a way that you can honor your relationships with them. As is clear from the foregoing, case studies vary in the degree to which they are aimed at presenting the perspectives of participants in the case; however, even when that is not a major aspect of what you are trying to do, your work on the case study would not have been possible without some assistance from participants, so you ought to recognize that relationship one way or another in your case study composition.

When you began your case study project, you needed to obtain access to sources of information. Some of the information you obtained was public information, but some of it was made available to you as a researcher (e.g., observation of meetings that were not publicly announced, official documents, office files). Someone helped you access that information, and you made either implicit or explicit promises to them about how you were going to use it. In your composition you need to be consistent with those promises.

As you worked on your case study project, you engaged in conversations with others involved in it. You may have requested that they allow you to interview them. You need to make sure that the use of their interviews in your composition is respectful of them. You probably also made some agreement regarding their participation in the interview. That agreement needs to be honored in the composition as well. Even if you only engaged in occasional conversations with some of your participants, the composition should reflect respectful and accurate use of the information and/or perspectives that you gained from those conversations. As was mentioned in Chapter 2, one way to assure respectful and accurate use is to engage participants in reviewing your composition and taking seriously their concerns and advice regarding it.

Neither **Johnston and Romzek** nor **Thompson** addresses the relationships of the authors with participants, so it is difficult to assess the degree to which their final compositions honor those relationships. Their silence on this topic may derive from public administration research traditions that do not include addressing it, but it could also be a way of respecting their privacy.

Finally, there may also be a need for you to protect some of the participants. Federal human subjects protocols do not require you to protect the anonymity of government officials, so you may feel that you are liberated from this concern if your project did not involve people normally considered members of a "vulnerable population." But your responsibility as a researcher goes beyond legal requirements. You should not include in your composition anything that, for example, would adversely affect a participant's relationship with his/her supervisor or coworkers. As a qualitative researcher you have been engaged with your participants, and you need to retain your sense of relationship with them as you consider what to reveal and what not to. In some cases you may even decide that being responsible means you must conceal the name and/or the location of the agencies that are treated in the case study. **Johnston and Romzek** and **Thompson** follow traditional academic compositional modes by making statements about unspecified parties' views (e.g., **Johnston and Romzek**, p. 390) and including unattributed quotes (e.g., **Johnston and Romzek**, p. 391). Other than that, neither article provides any evidence that the authors felt a need write their case studies with a concern about protecting individuals or agencies.

## Conclusion

This chapter described how to do a journal-article-length case study in public administration. The case study is among the most popular research approaches in public administration, but many articles that claim to be case studies are utilizing a very loose definition of that term. There are many definitions and many kinds of case studies.

The exemplar articles used in this chapter provide assistance in understanding how to do a public administration case study, but they are not perfect models. No case study is. There are many ways to do a case study. Regardless of the approach you take, though, you will need to do a number of things addressed in this chapter, among them identifying your case, justifying your case study, designing your case study, addressing and preparing for the logistical challenges you will face, gathering and/or creating your data, organizing that data, analyzing it, and writing your composition. Although these things sound like they may take place in a rather linear, step-by-step fashion, you will find that the relationships among them are recursive and multilateral. You may also want to do some of the things described in earlier chapters. Qualitative interviewing (whether utilizing narrative inquiry or not) and participant-observation field research (whether organized as an ethnographic approach or not) are very commonly among the data gathering procedures utilized in case study approaches.

Discovering the specific shape that your case study takes can be an interesting aspect of this approach to public administration research. At times it may feel like you are not making progress, but if you keep with it you will find that it is both possible and exciting to move from the idea of doing a case study to completing a case study composition.

## Notes

1. It is also a common approach to teaching, but this chapter will not deal with case studies as an approach to teaching.

2. The National Performance Review was a Clinton administration initiative aimed at "reinventing government."

3. I should admit that I also have fallen short in this respect. In my case study of Spokane solid waste policymaking, I did not report enough about this. Upon reflection, I think I was reluctant to report much about my relationships with people involved in the case because I feared that it would undermine my credibility as a researcher. At the time I did not have sufficient appreciation of the qualitative research tradition and the positive value it places on engaged and respectful relationships with participants.

4. Public administration case studies that demonstrate more creative and/or literary writing techniques are often used as teaching cases. R.J. Stillman II's *Public Administration: Concepts and Cases* (2005), for example, is a fine collection of quite readable teaching cases.

## Exercises

1. Find an article in a recent (last five years) professional journal that either says it is a case study or that you think qualifies as one. Write a list of explanations (at least three) for why you think it is a case study (or is not, if it claims to be and you disagree).

2. Find a case study (article or book length) and, using the characteristics discussed in this chapter, decide what kind of case study it is. Explain the grounds on which you made that decision.

3. Suggest a research topic that you think could be addressed using a case study approach. Explain what aspects of the topic could best be examined using a case study. Why would other approaches not be as good a way to examine those aspects?

4. Using the guidance provided in Box 5.2 identify, justify and frame a potential case study proposal.

5. Using Box 5.4 as a reference, write a plan for addressing the logistical challenges that you might face in doing the potential case study proposed in Exercise #4.

6. Examine a published case study (perhaps the one you used for Exercises #1 and/or #2) and, using Box 5.6 as a framework, describe the analytical activities you think went into it.

7. Reviewing published case studies (or other qualitative research publications), find good examples of:
   a. using nontraditional compositional structure
   b. being open about the role of researcher as interpreter
   c. disclosing the relationship between the researcher and other participants
   d. presenting the voice of participants
   e. thick description

## Recommended Readings

Creswell, J.W. 1998. Data collection. Chapter 7 in *Qualitative Inquiry and Research Design: Choosing Among Five Traditions*. Thousand Oaks, CA: Sage Publications.

Morse, Janice M. and Lyn Richards. 2002. Coding. Chapter 6 in *README FIRST for a User's Guide to Qualitative Methods*. Thousand Oaks, CA: Sage Publications.

## Recommended Web Site

Garson, David. Syllabus on Case Study Research. College of Humanities and Social Sciences, North Carolina State University. http://www2.chass.ncsu.edu/garson/ pa765/cases.htm.

## Additional Journal Article Examples of Case Studies

Corder, J.K., and S.M. Hoffmann. 2004. Privatizing federal credit programs: Why Sallie Mae? *Public Administration Review,* 64(2): 180–91.
Keast, R., M.P. Mandell, K. Brown, and G. Woolcock. 2004. Network structures: Working differently and changing expectations. *Public Administration Review,* 64(3): 363–71.
Mahler, J., and P.M. Regan. 2002. Learning to govern online: Federal agency Internet use. *The American Review of Public Administration,* 32(3): 326–49.
Mareschal, P.M. 2003. Solving problems and transforming relationships: The bifocal approach to mediation. *The American Review of Public Administration,* 33(4): 423–48.
Romzek, B.S., and M.J. Dubnick. 1987. Accountability in the public sector: Lessons from the *Challenger* tragedy. *Public Administration Review,* 47(3): 227–38.
Smith, R.W. 2003. Enforcement or ethical capacity: Considering the role of state ethics commissions at the millennium. *Public Administration Review,* 63(3): 283–95.
Stewart, J., and P. Kringas. 2003. Change management—strategy and values in six agencies from the Australian public service. *Public Administration Review,* 63(6): 675–88.
Thurmaier, K., and C. Wood. 2002. Interlocal agreements as overlapping social networks: Picket-fence regionalism in metropolitan Kansas City. *Public Administration Review,* 62(5): 585–98.
Townsend, W.A. 2004. Systems changes associated with criminal justice treatment networks. *Public Administration Review,* 64(5): 607–17.
Van Slyke, D.M., and C.A. Hammonds. 2003. The privatization decision: Do public managers make a difference? *The American Review of Public Administration,* 33(2): 146–63.

## Book Length Examples of Case Studies

Allison, G. 1971. *Essence of Decision: Explaining the Cuban Missile Crisis.* Boston: Little, Brown.
Luton, L.S. 1996. *The Politics of Garbage: A Community Perspective on Solid Waste Policy Making.* Pittsburgh, PA: University of Pittsburgh Press.
Selznick, P. 1949. *TVA and the Grass Roots: A Study in the Sociology of Formal Organization.* Berkeley: University of California Press.
Whyte, W.F. 1943. *Street Corner Society: The Social Structure of an Italian Slum.* Chicago: University of Chicago Press.

## References

Altheide, D., M. Coyle, K. DeVriese, and C. Schneider. 2008. Emergent qualitative document analysis. In *Handbook of Emergent Methods,* ed. S.N. Hesse-Biber and P. Leavy, 127–51. New York: Guilford Press.

## 156   CHAPTER 5

Berg, B.L. 2004. *Qualitative Research Methods for the Social Sciences.* 5th ed. Boston: Pearson Education.

Creswell, J.W. 1998. *Qualitative Inquiry and Research Design: Choosing Among Five Traditions.* Thousand Oaks, CA: Sage Publications.

Denzin, N.K. 1989. *Interpretive Interactionism.* Newbury Park, CA: Sage Publications.

Feldman, M.S., K. Skoldberg, R. Brown, and D. Horner. 2004. Making sense of stories: A rhetorical approach to narrative analysis. *Journal of Public Administration Research and Theory,* 14(2): 147–70.

Fischer, F., and J. Forester, eds. 1993. *The Argumentative Turn in Policy Analysis and Planning.* Durham, NC: Duke University Press.

Fox, Charles J., and Hugh M. Miller. 1996. *Postmodern Public Administration: Toward discourse.* Thousand Oaks, CA: Sage Publications.

Jensen, J.L., and R. Rodgers. 2001. Cumulating the intellectual gold of case study research. *Public Administration Review,* 61(2): 235–46.

Luton, L.S. 1996. *The Politics of Garbage: A Community Perspective on Solid Waste Policy Making.* Pittsburgh, PA: University of Pittsburgh Press.

March, J. 1981. Footnotes to organizational change. *Administrative Science Quarterly,* 26: 563–77.

Morse, Janice M., and Lyn Richards. 2002. *README FIRST for a User's Guide to Qualitative Methods.* Thousand Oaks, CA: Sage Publications.

Prior, L. 2008. Researching documents: Emergent methods. In *Handbook of Emergent Methods,* ed. S.N. Hesse-Biber and P. Leavy, 111–26. New York: Guilford Press.

Richards, Lyn, and Janice M. Morse. 2002. *README FIRST for a User's Guide to Qualitative Methods.* Thousand Oaks, CA: Sage Publications.

Richardson, L. 2003. Writing: A method of inquiry. In *Collecting and Interpreting Qualitative Materials,* ed. N.K. Denzin and Y.S. Lincoln, 499–541. Thousand Oaks, CA: Sage Publications.

Richardson, L. 2000. Writing: A method of inquiry. In *Handbook of Qualitative Research,* ed. N.K. Denzin and Y.S. Lincoln, 923–48. Thousand Oaks, CA: Sage Publications.

Romzek, B.S., and M.J. Dubnick. 1987. Accountability in the public sector: Lessons from the *Challenger* tragedy. *Public Administration Review,* 47(3): 227–38.

Schwandt, T.A. 2001. *Dictionary of Qualitative Inquiry.* 2d ed. Thousand Oaks, CA: Sage Publications.

Stake, R.E. 1995. *The Art of Case Study Research.* Thousand Oaks, CA: Sage Publications.

———. 2003. Case studies. In *Strategies of Qualitative Inquiry,* ed. N.K. Denzin and Y.S. Lincoln, 134–64. Thousand Oaks, CA: Sage Publications.

Stein, H. 1952. On public administration and public administration cases. In *Public Administration and Policy Development,* ed. H. Stein. New York: Harcourt Brace Jovanovich.

Stillman, R.J., II. 2005. *Public Administration: Concepts and Cases.* 8th ed. New York: Houghton Mifflin.

Word, L.A., and R.O. Kroger. 2000. *Doing Discourse Analysis: Methods for Studying Action in Talk and Text.* Thousand Oaks, CA: Sage Publications.

Yin, R.K. 1989. *Case Study Research: Design and Methods.* Rev. ed. Newbury Park, CA: Sage Publications.

———. 1993. *Applications of Case Study Research.* Newbury Park, CA: Sage Publications.

# Conclusion

This book is about taking qualitative research more seriously. Public administration journal articles that do not depend upon quantitative data are most often not qualitative research articles either. Qualitative research approaches are systematic research approaches. They require extensive preparation, genuine engagement, thoughtful analysis, and respectful presentation.

There is a long tradition of nonquantitative and qualitative research in public administration, but that tradition has not included enough conscientious attention to how to do systematic, carefully documented, and accountably presented qualitative research. The labels "semistructured interviews" and "case study" have too often been placed on public administration publications that did not take their approach to research very seriously. Although "narrative inquiry" has a more specific meaning in our field, it is often confused with "narrative analysis," a label that has been applied to a wide variety of freewheeling research approaches that interpreted a wide variety of "texts."

As I said in the first chapter, there are two rather basic reasons for doing qualitative research. The first reason is the kind of knowledge that is gained through qualitative approaches. Qualitative research is situated research, taking place in a specific location (or set of locations). For example, M. Baker-Boosamra, J.A. Guevara, and D.L. Balfour (2006) went to El Salvador to interview people about service learning in an international setting. J. Heyman (1995, 2001, 2002) did his ethnographic research along the U.S.–Mexico border. The lessons learned from such situated research are not generalizable, but they are transferable.

Qualitative research seeks to better understand a situation from an insider perspective, learning from insiders through interviews, observation, and a variety of other data collection and generation techniques. As the chapter on narrative inquiry showed, M.H. Vickers (2005) interviewed people with invisible diseases to better understand how those diseases affected their work experiences. S. Maynard-Moody and M. Musheno (2000) had cops, teachers, and counselors relate stories of their work world to better understand how they utilized discretion in making decisions.

Qualitative research retains contextual perspective as it tries to understand the world of public administration. Heyman (2001) put his understanding of Immigration and Naturalization Service classification practices in the larger context of U.S. immigration and nationality laws, labor markets, and societal treatment of immigrants. J.R. Thompson (1999) placed the reinvention labs and the National Performance Review into a larger context of administrative reform.

Qualitative research not only places its work in a larger context; it also gets up close and personal. It often delves into the tacit knowledge that people have about their experiences. In this book, Vickers's (2005) work is probably the best example. She delved in a very personal way into the work world experiences of those with invisible diseases. Similarly, S.K. Okamoto (2001) learned about the impact of fear on collaboration efforts by interviewing practitioners.

Bringing together the larger context and the individual perspective contributes to making qualitative research holistic. The narrative inquiry chapter contains excellent examples of this, demonstrating how the whole gives meaning to its parts (and vice versa). The exploration of stories requires an examination of the how the whole story is composed of its parts—and how the whole story contributes to the meanings we derive about its parts.

The second basic reason that public administration researchers engage in qualitative approaches is that they provide avenues through which to engage in a meaningful, authentic, and productive way with practitioners. M.A. Lyles and I.I. Mitroff (1980) used a semistructured interview approach to draw out managers about their perceptions of the formulation process related to problems that had significant impacts on their organizations. They knew that a written questionnaire would not provide the flexibility they needed—the opportunity to seek explanations and to probe in ways that would help their interviewees become more "aware of their own problem-formulation process" (p. 105). They treated their interviewees as sources of understanding, not just sources of data. In developing such relationships with administrators, clients, and citizens, public administration researchers are more likely to do research that is interesting not only to researchers but also to others. Those relationships should also improve the quality of the understanding gained through the research.

Each of the specific approaches addressed in this book are aimed in their own way at learning from others. As the chapter on qualitative interviewing suggested, that approach is well designed to better understand other points of view and the meanings that others attach to situations, settings, events, etc., and to integrate multiple perspectives. Narrative inquiry adds focus and depth to interviewing by taking deliberate steps to develop a more holistic perspective—using stories to incorporate the flow of time and the complexity of relationships and group and institutional dynamics. Ethnographic approaches add to interviewing and narrative inquiry, perspectives gained through direct in-the-field observation and engagement. Case study approaches involve interviewing, observation, and analysis of the roles that documents play in the dynamics of the situation, providing a kind of triangulation on the information and insights gained. It was that kind of triangulation that brought the gap between rhetoric and reality into focus for J.M. Johnston and B.S. Romzek (1999).

There are many ways to do qualitative research. D.E. McNabb (2002) identifies six. D. Yanow and P. Shwartz-Shea (2006), while they do not attempt to categorize the approaches included in their book, include among them several not addressed in this book—e.g., value-critical policy analysis, interpretive content analysis, and the semiotics of space. Moreover, there is no single recipe for any particular qualitative research approach. I have tried to design the chapters in this book to provide helpful guidelines while leaving room for the readers to develop their own styles within those guidelines. To the degree that the chapters are seen as recipes, please read them with the attitude my sister suggests should be taken toward food recipes: They are only one cook's idea of how to do it.

The exemplar articles in each chapter give some idea of the stylistic differences available within the approaches described in this book. Take, for example, narrative inquiry. The rhetorical approach taken by M.S. Feldman et al. (2004) aimed at revealing the unstated aspects of arguments presented through stories, but the hermeneutical approach taken by Vickers (2005) aimed at giving voice to a marginalized group, and the story-based research of Maynard-Moody and Musheno (2000) aimed at understanding the perspective of street-level workers regarding the proper use of their discretion. Feldman et al. reformulated stories into arguments. Vickers shared stories that were incomplete ("antenarratives"). Maynard-Moody and Musheno deliberately prepared their interviewees to tell complete stories, then contrasted the general perspective those stories shared with the expectations of public administration literature.

There are many ways we could enhance and improve our use of qualitative research approaches. We should begin by becoming more familiar with the multidisciplinary conversation about qualitative research. Other fields, especially other professional fields such as social work and health services administration, include much from which we could gain. One such aspect that was alluded to in this text involves approaches to composing our re-presentation of the perspectives of others. Public administration qualitative researchers have not been very imaginative in finding alternative composition forms to better capture the voices of those we interview, observe, and engage.

In sum, as this book suggests, and as utilization of the approaches in this book will further demonstrate, qualitative research adds valuable perspectives to public administrators' understanding of their work and its impacts. Of course this is not the first book to suggest the value of qualitative research, and it will not, and should not, be the last textbook on qualitative research approaches in public administration. It is, I hope, a valuable contribution to the literature, but it only addresses four qualitative research approaches and it limits its treatment of those to work that resulted in journal articles. Much qualitative research results in book-length publications.

I look forward to further developments in qualitative research approaches in public administration, to improvements in our research approaches, additional contributions to our understanding of the field, and resulting improvements in the practice of public administration. When we attend carefully to public administration practitioners, we should be able to do research that they find relevant. If we help them become more reflective about their practice, their approaches to their work challenges should improve. Moreover, as we learn from others how they are impacted by public administration and incorporate their perspectives into innovations designed to improve our service to them, public administration should get better and better.

If you accept the challenge of taking qualitative research more seriously, I hope to hear from you about your approaches and your experiences. Together, we will improve our research approaches and our field's understanding of the practice of public administration. It will be a great collective adventure.

## References

Baker-Boosamra, M., J.A. Guevara, and D.L. Balfour. 2006. From service to solidarity: Evaluation and recommendations for international service learning. *Journal of Public Administration Education*, 12(4): 479–500.

Feldman, M.S., K. Sköldberg, R. Brown, and D. Horner. 2004. Making sense of stories: A rhetorical approach to narrative analysis. *Journal of Public Administration Research and Theory*, 14(2): 147–70.

Heyman, J. McC. 1995. Putting power in the anthropology of bureaucracy: The Immigration and Naturalization Service at the Mexico–United States border. *Current Anthropology*, 36(2): 261–87.

———. 2001. Class and classification at the U.S.–Mexico border. *Human Organization*, 60(2): 128–40.

———. 2002. U.S. immigration officers of Mexican ancestry as Mexican Americans, citizens, and immigration police. *Current Anthropology*, 43(3): 479–96.

Johnston, J.M., and B.S. Romzek. 1999. Contracting and accountability in state Medicaid reform: Rhetoric, theories, and reality. *Public Administration Review*, 59(5): 383–99.

Lyles, M.A., and I.I. Mitroff. 1980. Organizational problem formulation: An empirical study. *Administrative Science Quarterly*, 25(1): 102–19.

Maynard-Moody, S., and M. Musheno. 2000. State agent or citizen agent: Two narratives of discretion. *Journal of Public Administration Research and Theory*, 10(2): 329–58.

McNabb, D.E. 2002. *Research Methods in Public Administration and Nonprofit Management: Quantitative and Qualitative Approaches*. Armonk, NY: M.E. Sharpe.

Okamoto, S.K. 2001. Interagency collaboration with high-risk gang youth. *Child and Adolescent Social Work Journal*, 18(1): 5–19.

Thompson, J.R. 1999. Devising administrative reform that works: The example of the reinvention lab program. *Public Administration Review*, 59(4): 283–92.

Vickers, M.H. 2005. Illness, work and organization: Postmodern perspectives, antenarratives and chaos narratives for the reinstatement of voice. *Tamara: Journal of Critical Postmodern Organization Science*, 3(2): 74–88.

Yanow, D., and P. Shwartz-Shea, eds. 2006. *Interpretation and Method: Empirical Research Methods and the Interpretive Turn*. Armonk, NY: M.E. Sharpe.

# Name Index

Abel, C.F., 8
Abolafia, M.Y., 7, 11
Adams, Guy B., 6–8
Akert, R.M., 40
Allcorn, S., 8
Altheide, D., 143
Amara, N., 13
Anders, K.K., 6
Angrosino, M., 89, 92
Archer, D., 40
Atkinson, P., 95, 107

Bailey, M., 7
Baker-Boosamra, 22, 23, 26–30, 32,
    34, 39–40, 42–46, 48, 157
Balfour, D.L., 22, 23, 26–30, 32, 34,
    39–40, 42–46, 48, 57, 157
Battistelli, F., 8
Beebe, J., 29
Beresford, A.D., 8
Berg, B.L., 21, 29, 32, 34–35, 34, 40,
    88, 150
Blumer, H., 111
Boje, D.M., 70-71
Bolton, M., 13–14
Box, Richard, 6
Brady, H.E., 4–5, 10–12
Brower, R.S., 7, 11
Brown, R., 55, 56, 58, 64–66, 68–72,
    75–76, 80–82, 143, 159–160
Burnier, D., 8
Carr, J.B., 7, 11

Chatman, S., 77
Cheedy, Jaja, 6
Chiseri-Strater, E., 105
Churchman, C.W., 42
Cimitile, C.J., 8
Clandinin, D.J., 61–62, 73, 77
Claunch, R., 55
Cleary, R.E., 5–7
Collier, D., 4–5, 10–11
Connell, R., 22
Connelly, F.M., 61, 73, 77
Cook, S.D.N., 12
Corbin, J., 110
Creswell, John W., 4, 88, 139
Czarniawska, B., 54, 57, 59–60

Denhardt, R.B., 8
Denzin, N.K., 13, 150
Diamond, M.A., 8
Dodge, J., 7, 54–55, 61
Douglas, J.D., 25

Elliott, J., 58–59, 61
Ely, M., 76
Emerson, R.M., 102, 106, 111, 115
Erlandson, David A., 10
Evans, K.G., 5–7

Farmer, David J., 9, 54–55
Felbinger, C.L., 7
Feldman, M.S., 55, 56, 58, 64–66,
    68–72, 75–76, 80–82, 143, 159–160

Ferris, J.A., 5
Fetterman, D.M., 88, 109
Fischer, F., 54–55, 143–144
Flick, U., 88
Foldy, E.G., 7, 55
Fontana, A., 25
Forester, J., 54, 143–144
Fox, Charles J., 9, 131
Frank, A.W., 70
Freeman, Ellen, 35
Fretz, R.I., 102, 106, 111, 115
Frey, J.H., 25

GAO, 10, 86, 89
Geertz, C., 11, 112
Gleason, G.R., 100
Godschalk, D.R., 8
Goffman, E., 25
Gore, Al, 11, 144–145
Gross, Terry, 35–37
Guba, E.G., 5
Gubrium, J.F., 22, 25
Guevara, J.A., 22, 23, 26–30, 32, 34,
    39–40, 42–46, 48, 157

Hammersley, M., 95, 107
Harmon, M.M., 8
Hendricks, J.J., 8
Herr, M., 56
Herzog, R.J., 8, 55
Heyman, Josiah McC., 86, 87–88, 90–
    94, 96–97, 99–101, 103, 107–108,
    110–111, 113–114, 116, 157–158
Holstein, J.A., 22, 25
Holzer, M., 7
Horner, D., 55, 56, 58, 64–66, 68–72,
    75–76, 80–82, 143, 159–160
Hummel, R.P., 7, 54
Hutchinson, J.R., 8

James, W., 10
Jensen, J.L., 127
Johnston, J.M., 121–127, 122,
    129–133, 137, 141–142, 145,
    147–150, 152, 159
Kamensky, J.M., 137

Kaufman, H., 86
Kelly, J., 8
Kelly, M., 7
Kettl, D.F., 141
King, C.S., 14
Kraemer, K.L., 5
Kroger, R.O., 143
Kvale, S., 26, 28–29, 38, 41, 47–48

Lamari, M., 13
Lan, Z., 5–6
Landry, R., 13
LeCompte, M.D., 87, 99
Lincoln, Y.S., 13
Lipskey, M., 86
Lott, John R., 11
Lowery, D., 5–7
Luton, L., 132
Lyles, M.A., 22, 23–24, 26–28, 30,
    40–42, 44, 46, 48, 158–159

Malinowski, B., 95
Mann, H.S., 8
March, J., 141
Mareschal, P.M., 8
Maynard-Moody, S., 7–8, 55–56, 55,
    58–62, 65–68, 72, 74–79, 81, 158,
    160
Mays de Pérez, K.A., 89, 92
McCurdy, H.E., 5–7
McNabb, D.E., 7, 10, 14, 159
McSwite, O.C., 9
Mesaros, W., 57
Miller, Hugh T., 6, 9, 131
Minieri, J., 56
Mitroff, I.I., 22, 23–24, 26–28, 30,
    40–42, 44, 46, 48, 158–159
Morgan, D.L., 40
Morse, J.M., 49, 138–139
Musheno, M., 8, 55–56, 55, 58–62,
    65–68, 72, 74–79, 81, 158,
    160
Nedovic-Budic, Z., 8

Okamoto, S.K., 22, 23, 26–27, 29–30,
    39–40, 43–44, 46, 48–49, 158

Orosz, J., 7
Ospina, S.M., 7, 54–56, 61

Perry, J.L., 5
Polkinghorne, D.E., 57–58, 60, 62
Prior, L., 143

Ragin, Charles, 4, 10, 12
Rao, S., 56
Research Center for Leadership
    in Action (Wagner/New York
    University), 56
Richards, Lyn, 49, 138–139, 146, 149
Ricotta, G., 8
Riessman, C.K., 62, 67–68, 70
Rivera, M., 14
Rockefeller Institute's State Capacity
    Study, 131
Rodgers, R., 127
Roe, E., 54–55
Romzek, B.S., 121–127, 122, 129–133,
    137, 141–142, 145, 147–150, 152,
    159
Rosiek, J., 61–62
Rossman, E.J., 23
Rubin, H.J., 7, 21, 23, 25, 29, 36, 38,
    40, 42, 45
Rubin, I.S., 7, 21, 23, 25, 29, 36, 38,
    40, 42, 45

Sandfort, J.R., 8
Schensul, J.J., 87, 99
Schmidt, Mary R., 7, 12
Schwandt, Thomas A., 135
Schwartz-Shea, P., 7–8
Scrimshaw, N.S., 100
Sementelli, A.J., 8
Shaw, L.L., 102, 106, 111, 115
Shields, P.M., 10
Shwartz-Shea, P., 159
Silverman, D., 8
Sköldberg, K., 55, 56, 58, 64–66,
    68–72, 75–76, 80–82, 143,
    159–160

Slotkin, B.J., 14
Spradley, J.P., 88–89
Stake, R.E., 125–126, 131, 138, 141–142
Stallings, R.A., 5–6
Steele, Karen Dorn, 136
Stein, H., 122–123
Stivers, C., 8
Stolcis, G., 13–14
Stone, D.A., 54–55
Stone-Mediatore, S., 61
Strauss, A., 110
Streib, G., 14
Sunstein, B.S., 105

Tausig, Jane, 35
Thatcher, D., 8
Thompson, J.R., 8, 121, 122, 123–127,
    129–133, 136–137, 141–142, 144,
    146–150, 152, 158

U.S. General Accounting Office
    (GAO) (now Government
    Accountability Office), 10, 86, 89

Van Maanen, J., 89, 102
Vickers, M.H., 8, 55, 56, 59–62,
    65–66, 68, 70–71, 73–76, 79–80,
    82, 158, 160

Waldo, D., 6
Wamsley, G.L., 8
Wanna, J., 8
Weiss, R.S., 22, 29, 31–32, 33, 35–36,
    37, 39–40
White, Jay D., 6–8, 55, 57
Wolf, J.F., 8
Word, L.A., 143

Yanow, D., 7–8, 12, 159
Yin, R.K., 123–124, 126–127, 130,
    141, 147–148

Zanetti, L.A., 8, 14

# Subject Index

Abstract theory, 111
Academic article formats. *See* Journal
 article formats
Action theory paradigm, 8
Adjudication Division, 132
Administrative ethnography, 89–90
Agency fear, 45
Analysis
 argument, 55–56
 data, 108–112, *109*, 138–142, *140*
 dialogic/performance, 67
 discourse, 55–56
 documents
  as actors, 142–145, *143*
  as social experience, 145
 interview, 41–45
 multiple units of, 126
 single units of, 126
 stories, 58, 67–72, *72*
 structural, 67–71
 thematic, 67
 types of, 67–71
Antenarratives, 66, 70–71, 79
Anti-Drug Abuse Act (1988), 85
Applied ethnography, 89–90
Applied research, 56
Argument analysis, 55–56
Audience
 case studies and, 146–147, *151*
 narrative inquiry and, 73, 75
 writing style and, 47
Autoethnography, 89–90

Berg's ten commandments of
 interviewing, 34, *34*

Case studies
 audience and, 146–147, *151*
 challenges of, 128, *128*
 collective, 126
 comparative, 127
 compositional techniques, 148–150,
  *151*
 data
  analyzing, 138–142, *140*
  collecting, 134–138
  creating, 134–138
  sources, 135–137, *137*
 defining, 122–126
 designing, 128–133, *128*
 documents, analyzing
  as actors, 142–145, *143*
  as social experience, 145
 embedded, 126
 exemplar articles, 121–127, *122*,
  129–133, 136–137, 141–142,
  145–150, 152, 158–159
 functions of, 128–129, *129*
 holistic, 126
 instrumental, 126
 intrinsic, 126
 journal article format, 147–148, *151*
 label, 3
 logistical issues and, 133–134, *134*
 longitudinal, 127

Case studies *(continued)*
  multiple, 126–128
  note taking in, 138
  overview, 121, 153
  patchwork, 127
  pre-post, 127
  privacy issues and, 152
  in public administration, 121, 131–
    132, 135–136, 144–145, 149–150
  quotations and, 150
  relationships in
    with audience, 146–147, *151*
    with participants, 151–152, *151*
  single, 126, 135
  snapshot, 127
  thick descriptions and, 150
  types of, 126–128
  utilizing, 14, 128–129, *129*
  value of, 13
  voice and, 149–150
Causation, 11–12
*Challenger* accident, 130
Chaos narrative, 70
Chronological compositional structure,
  148
Co-constitution, 71–72
Coding transcripts, 43–44, 111–112
Collaboration, 43–44
Collecting data, 104–108, 134–138
Collective case studies, 126
Comparative case studies, 127
Communication, 43–45
Compositional structure. *See* Journal
  article formats
Compositional techniques, 148–150,
  *151*
Conclusion section of journal articles,
  47
Context, 10, 158
Contracting for social services
  (Kansas), 122–124, 141–142, 145
Convenience sampling, 39
Conversation, 21–22, 24
Cooperation, 43
Creating data, 104–108, 134–138
Credibility, 44

Data
  analyzing, 108–112, *109*, 138–142, *140*
  coding, 43–44, 111–112
  collecting, 104–108, 134–138
  creating, 104–108, 134–138
  interview, 37–41
  sources, 106–108, *108*, 135–137, *137*
Designing
  case studies, 128–133, *128*
  ethnographic research, 95–97, *98*,
    99–102
  interviewing, 26–28
  narrative inquiry, 63–67, *64*
Dialogic/performance analysis, 67
Discourse analysis, 55–56
Diversity, 6
Documentary evidence, 106–108
Documents, analyzing
  as actors, 142–145, *143*
  as social experience, 145

Educational ethnography, 89–90
Embedded case designs, 126
Emplotted narratives, 60. *See also*
  Narrative inquiry
Enthymeme, 69–70
Ethnographic research
  administrative, 89–90
  applied, 89–90
  autoethnography, 89–90
  challenges of, *98*, 99–100
  data
    analyzing, 108–112, *109*
    collecting, 104–108, 135
    creating, 104–108
    sources, 106–108, *108*
  defining, 87–89
  designing, 95–97, *95*, 99–102
  educational, 89–90
  exemplar articles, *86*, 87–88, 90–94,
    96–97, 99–101, 103, 107–108,
    110–111, 113–114, 116, 157–158
  fieldwork in, 100–101, 106
  functions of, 90–92, *91*
  journal article format, 101–102, 112–
    115, *114*

Ethnographic research *(continued)*
  logistical issues and, 102–104, *103*
  medical, 89–90
  note taking in, 105–106
  observation in, 105
  overview, 85–87, 116–117
  in public administration, 10, 85–86,
    90, 113
  selecting approach, 90–95, *91*
  types of, 89–90
  U.S. General Accounting Office, 10
  traditional, 89
  urban, 89–90
  utilizing, 90–92, *91*
Evocative representations, 149–150
Exemplar articles
  case studies, 121–127, *122*, 129–133,
    136–137, 141–142, 145–150,
    152, 158–159
  ethnographic research, *86*, 87–88,
    90–94, 96–97, 99–101, 103,
    107–108, 110–111, 113–114,
    116, 157–158
  functions of, 15
  interviewing, *22*, 23–24, 26–30, 32,
    34, 39–46, 48, 157–159
  narrative inquiry, 55–56, *55*, 58–62,
    64–72, 74–82, 143, 158–160
  qualitative research and, 159–160
  theory behind, 15
Experiential knowledge, 61–62

Fear, 43, 45
Fieldwork, 100–101, 106
Findings section of journal articles,
  47
Flashback, 60
Focus group technique, 39–40
Follow-up questions, 30–31
Forms, narrative, 57, 73, 76
Fragmented stories. *See* Antenarratives

GAO, 10, 86, 89
Grounded theory, 71, 110–111

Holistic case designs, 126

Immigration and Naturalization
  Service (INS), 87, 90–92, 97,
    100–104
Instrumental case studies, 126
Internal Review Board, 32
Interpretive approaches, 57
Interview guide, preparing, 28–31, *29,
  30*
Interviewees
  panel of, 39–40
  post-interview anxieties of, 66
  pre-interview briefing of, 33, *33*
  quotations of, 48–49, 150
  relationship of interviewer with,
    25–26, 33, 35, 73
  selection of, 24–25, 27–28
Interviewers, good, 38–39, 41
Interviewing. *See also* Narrative
    inquiry
  Berg's ten commandments of, 34, *34*
  conversation versus, 21–22
  defining, 21–26
  designing, 26–28
  exemplar articles, *22*, 23–24, 26–30,
    32, 34, 39–46, 48, 157–159
  functions of, 25–26, *25*
  interview
    actual interview, 34–37, *34, 35,
      36, 37*
    analyzing, 41–45
    data, 37–41
    guide, preparing, 28–31, *29, 30*
    interviewer, good, 38–39, 41
    questions, 28–31, *29, 30*
    situation, preparing, 32–34, *33*
  interviewee selection for, 24–25,
    27–28
  journal article format, 45–49
  note taking in, 40
  overview, 21, 49–50
  panel of interviewees for, 39–40
  in public administration, 23–26,
    49–50
  qualitative research versus, 21–22
  relationship with interviewees and,
    25–26, 33, 35, 73

Interviewing *(continued)*
  sampling, 39
  semistructured interviewing versus,
    23–24
  single case design and, 135
  site selection for, 27–28
  structured survey interviewing
    versus, 22–23
  topic selection for, 26–27
  utilizing, 25–26, *25*
Interviews, 34–37, *34, 35, 36, 37. See
  also* Interviewing
Intrinsic case studies, 126
Introduction section of journal articles,
  46, 113

Journal article formats
  case studies, 147–148, *151*
  ethnographic research, 101–102,
    112–115, *114*
  interviewing, 45–49
  narrative inquiry, 76–81, *78*
  stories in, incorporating, 76–81, *78*
  story-based, 114–115, *114*
  thematic, 114–115, *114*

Kairotic time, 60
Kettl model, 141–142

Leadership for a Changing World
  (LCW), 56
Linear-analytic compositional
  structure, 148
Literary critique, 57
Literature review section of journal
  articles, 46, 113–114
Logistical issues
  case studies and, 133–134, *134*
  ethnographic research and, 102–104,
    *103*
  narrative inquiry and, 65
Longitudinal case study, 127

Manuscript, composing. *See* Journal
  article formats
March's theoretical framework, 141

Media reports, 135–136
Medicaid, 122–124, 141, 145
Medical ethnography, 89–90
Methods section of journal articles,
  46–47, 136–137
Multiple case studies and designs,
  126–128
Multiple conjunctural causation, 12
Multiple units of analysis, 126

Narrative inquiry
  antenarratives and, 66, 70–71, 79
  in applied research, 56
  arguments for using, 59–60, *63*
  audience and, 73, 75
  challenges of, 64–66, *64*
  defining, 57–59
  designing, 63–67, *64*
  enthymeme and, 69–70
  exemplar articles, 55–56, *55*, 58–62,
    64–72, 74–82, 143, 158–160
  forms of narratives and, 57, 73,
    76
  functions of, 59–63
  interviewing and, 63
  journal article formats, 76–81, *78*
  literary genres and, 70–71
  logistical issues and, 65
  overview, 54–56, 81
  plots and, 58, 79
  in policy analysis, 54–55
  privacy issues and, 65
  in public administration, 54–55, 57,
    62–63, 73, 77
  signature and, 73–75
  stories
    analyzing, 58, 67–72, *72*
    incorporating in journal article
      format, 76–81, *78*
    interpreting, 59
    re-presenting, 73–81
    text, composing, 73–81, *74*
    temporality and, 60–61
    utilizing, 59–63
    voice and, 73–74, 76
National Performance Review, 144

New York Regional Office/Veterans Benefit Administration, 144
Nodes, 43
Nonverbal communication, 40
Note taking
  in case studies, 138
  in ethnographic research, 105–106
  in interviewing, 40
NUD*IST (Non-numerical Unstructured Data Indexing, Searching, and Theoretical) software, 70

Observation, 105
Organizational files, 106

Panel of interviewees, 39–40
Patchwork case study, 127
Pattern matching logic, 141
Plots, 58, 79
Policy analysis, 54–55
Post-interview anxieties of interviewees, 66
Postmodernism, 8–9
Pre-interview briefing of interviewees, 33, 33
Pre-post case study, 127
Privacy issues, 65, 152
Probes, 30, 31
ProQuest search (2006), 85
Public administration
  case studies in, 121, 131–132, 135–136, 144–145, 149–150
  context of research and, 10
  ethnographic research in, 10, 85–86, 90, 113
  interviewing in, 23–26, 49–50
  narrative inquiry in, 54–55, 57, 62–63, 73, 77
  nonquantitative research in, 157
  postmodernism in, 8–9
  qualitative research in, 3, 5–10, 13–14, 157–161
Purposive sampling, 39

Qualitative case studies. See Case studies
Qualitative interviewing. See Interviewing
Qualitative research. See also specific type
  action theory paradigm and, 8
  causation and, 11–12
  components of, 3
  context and, 10, 158
  defining, 4–5
  diversity and, 6
  exemplar articles and, 159–160
  functions of, 9–14
  gap between what practitioners see and what academic research can deliver, 14
  goals of, 9–10
  improving, 160–161
  interviewing versus, 21–22
  knowledge sought by, 9–10, 12–13
  labels related to, 3
  literature of, 7–8
  methods of, various, 159
  overview, 3–4, 157–161
  in public administration, 3, 5–10, 13–14, 157–161
  quantitative research versus, 4–5, 10–11, 13
  theoretical perspectives and, 8
  thick descriptions and, 10–12
  utilizing, 7–8, 158–159
  value of, 12–14, 160
Quantitative research
  knowledge sought by, 9
  qualitative research versus, 4–5, 10–11, 13
  single case design and, 135
  utilizing, 6
Quest narrative, 70
Questions, interview, 28–31, 29, 30
Quotations of interviewees, 48–49, 150

Repackaging coded transcripts, 43–44
Reports, 107, 135–136
Restitution narrative, 70

Rhetorical analytical approach, 69
Rockefeller Institute's State Capacity
    Study, 131

Sampling, 39
Self-knowledge, 62
Semistructured interview, 3, 23–24
Signature, 73–75
Single case designs, 126, 135
Single unit analysis, 126
Situation, interview, 32–34, *33*
Skilled nursing facility (SNF), 124
Snapshot case study, 127
SNF, 124
Snowball sampling, 39
Solid waste policymaking (Spokane),
    132–133, 136, 144
Solidarity, 43, 45
Sources of data, 106–108, *108*, 135–
    137, *137*
State Capacity Study (Rockefeller
    Institute), 131
Stories. *See* Narrative inquiry
Story-based essay, 114–115, *114*
Structural analysis, 67–71
Structured survey interviewing, 22–23
Superfund, 23
Survey research, 134
Syllogisms, 70

Tacit knowledge, 12–13
Tales from the field, 57
Tales of the field, 57
Telephone interviews, 35
Temporality, 60–61
Text, composing, 73–81, *74*
Thematic analysis, 67
Thematic essay, 114–115, *114*
Theoretical perspectives, 8
Theory building compositional
    structure, 148
Theory-guided approach, 71
Thick descriptions, 10–12, 150
Traditional ethnography, 89
Transcriptions, 40–41, 43–44, 111–112

Urban ethnography, 89–90
U.S. General Accounting Office (now
    U.S. Government Accountability
    Office), 10, 86, 89

Veterans Services Division, 132
Visual analysis, 67
Voice, 73–74, 76, 149–150
    case studies and, 149–150
    narrative inquiry and, 73–74, 76

Writing style, 47–48
Written records, 106–107

# About the Author

**Larry S. Luton** is professor and director of public administration at Eastern Washington University where he teaches courses in research approaches, public policy and administrative law. His special interests include qualitative research approaches, public administration theory, and environmental policy administration. A member of the American Society for Public Administration for over 25 years, he has served in numerous leadership positions for that organization. He also serves on the editorial board for *Administrative Theory & Praxis*.